Born into Love

The Unconditional Love of Grandparents
Raising Their Grandchildren

Peggy J. O'Connor

PublishAmerica
Baltimore

First printing

Hardcover 978-1-4512-1520-5
Softcover 978-1-4489-4299-2
PUBLISHED BY PUBLISHAMERICA, LLLP
www.publishamerica.com
Baltimore

Printed in the United States of America

Dedicated to the grandmothers and grandfathers around the world, who are taking their grandchildren in when their parents can no longer handle the responsibility, giving them the unconditional love they need to grow into stable adults, and the many agencies trying desperately to help them.

This book is written to alert the public and government officials to the epidemic of grandparents taking on the parental responsibility for their grandchildren. There are tremendous needs not being met for these grandfamilies. Legislators need to write new law to extend legal standing to the grandparents who are sacrificing everything to give their grandchildren a healthy and stable environment to grow in. Quotes from studies, articles, or books are the work of the individuals who wrote them and not the work of this author. Numbers are changing as this book is written and the writer cannot guarantee the latest figures.

The path we take in life does not always follow our dreams and our goals. Some say 75% of what we accomplish is due to planning and the other 25% is luck and if you don't have that 25% of luck, you may not reach your goals. This book is not an official study of Grandparents Raising Grandchildren, but rather a compilation of information to educate the world of the massive growth of Grandfamilies and the challenges they face. Statistics are changing daily and new studies are being conducted with the Internet a wealth of information. This should only be the beginning.

A Child is Born

Born out of love are these babes

Not knowing who they can count on

Into the "system" they must go

Unless they are born again

Into the unconditional love of their grandparents

Born into love at last

Grandfamilies

It's not planned nor anticipated. It destroys some dreams while living another. It steals health, wealth, and esteem. It is the fate of Grandparents Raising Grandchildren. When asked if they would change anything, the consistent response is: "Of course not, they're my grandchildren".

Millions of grandmothers who have finally reached the time in their lives when they can look at taking care of themselves, find themselves back in the role of mother and may sacrifice their own care to meet the child's needs. Socializing with peers becomes nonexistent and many are shunned by family and friends who do not want to be bothered. It can be a hard, lonely existence.

The vast majority of grandchildren who come to grandparents have been abandoned, abused, neglected and unwanted. They carry the baggage with them of Post Traumatic Stress Disorder, Attachment Disorder, brain damage from crack cocaine moms, and many with ADD/ADHD from mothers who abused substances while pregnant.

Society must acknowledge that many grandparents are not living the anticipated lives of retirees when they find themselves taking the responsibility of a second family, their grandchildren. In the past 10 years, the term Grandfamilies became descriptive of a viable family unit though the system does not recognize them as such, and opportunities afforded to other family groups are not accessible unless the grandparents are living at or below the poverty level.

A Changing Society

It is estimated by the U.S. Census Bureau that approximately six million children are living in grandparent-headed households, 1.5 million more than the last census. Grandparents range in age from 35 to 85, either working towards retirement or attempting to live on retirement funds while meeting the needs of children now in their care. An average of 20% live in poverty. Federal grants only allow for approximately 10% of kinship care grants to be allotted to grandparents raising grandchildren and since approximately 80% of them work and own homes, they cannot qualify. Savings, retirement funds, downsized housing and increased health care are accepted challenges for these grandparents.

The grandparents cross over all lines of ethnicity, race, religion, and socio-economic parameters. With approximately 80% of the grandparents handling the financial needs of the children themselves, those at the higher end of the scale face no significant problems. Those in the poverty level are helped by entitlement programs. The middle income group is most affected as they are forced to either work longer to meet the financial needs, or use personal savings and/or retirement funds to care for the children. This may necessitate ignoring their own needs, hopes and dreams in order to accomplish meeting the needs of the children.

Ethnicity depends on the geographic area and rural versus urban areas. Some grandchildren are placed in the foster care system, some are adopted, and many are under temporary guardianship. A large number of grandparents take the grandchildren in on an informal basis in an attempt to help their children and protect the grandchildren. Parents of these children are unable to be responsible for their own children due to mental illness, physical illness, substance abuse, economic hardships or incarceration. Some of the children retain a "homeless" designation which allows for transportation and meal assistance through the schools.

Number of children being raised by grandparents, per state.

State	Count	State	Count
Arizona	52,210	Alabama	56,369
Alaska	5,419	Arkansas	33,618
California	625,934	Colorado	28,524
Connecticut	39,797	Delaware	13,726
Florida	258,982	Georgia	92,265
Hawaii	38,051	Idaho	8,110
Illinois	213,465	Indiana	81,537
Iowa	22,985	Kansas	17,873
Kentucky	57,141	Louisiana	117,859
Maine	9,276	Massachusetts	67,781
Michigan	70,044	Minnesota	17,682
Mississippi	48,061	Missouri 7	7,857
Montana	9,526	Nebraska	8,454
Nevada	30,580	New York	297,239
New Jersey	127,263	New Hampshire	10,119
New Mexico	41,085	North Carolina	79,810
North Dakota	3,901	Ohio	157,298
Oklahoma	57,601	Oregon	37,536
Pennsylvania	164,354	Puerto Rico	133,881
Rhode Island	11,231	South Carolina	51,775
South Dakota	8,340	Tennessee	61,252

Texas	448,439	Vermont	1,934
Virgin Islands	4,471	Virginia	59,464
Utah	31,099	Washington	35,341
West Virginia	24,276	Wisconsin	23,687
Wyoming	5,150		

Note: these numbers obtained from Generations United and are based on earlier census. Numbers have been growing steadily and 2010 Census anticipates approximately 6 million children being raised on grandparent headed households.

According to the U.S. Census Bureau, the number of children under 18 living in grandparent-headed house-holds increased markedly, from 2.2 million (or 3.2 percent of children) in 1970 to approximately 4 million (or 5.5 percent of children) in 1997. While many grandparent-headed households also include at least one of the grandchild's parents, the fastest-growing type of grandparent-headed household, since 1990, is more likely to be comprised of grandparents and their grandchildren, without the grandchild's parents. Some refer to these households as "skipped-generation" households. By 2000, approximately 2.4 million grandparents were responsible for most of the basic needs of their grandchildren.[5]

It is noticeable that grandparents as parents were not included in the National Census until 2000. Federal funding to states only started in 2005 and only 10% of funding is relegated to grandparents with the remaining 90% to kinship care. The overall feeling is that the grandparents should be able to handle the financial responsibilities of raising their grandchildren. If grandchildren are kept in foster care programs, grandparents can receive medical assistance as well as financial assistance, and many states offer parenting classes to help the grandparents adjust to raising a new generation. If the grandparents adopt the grandchildren, acceptance by state medical programs is usually prohibited by the retirement income.

Overall, drug and alcohol abuse are the primary reasons for children being placed in the grandparents home. Secondary is incarceration. Most grandparents look at the placement as temporary in the hopes that their children will get their lives together enough to resume their parenting rolls. Unfortunately this is increasingly not the case. Addiction problems and continued incidents with the law, preclude the parents from achieving goals of raising their children. If they do achieve their goals, the children are again removed from the home where they know security and go back to the parents. Substance abusers tend to go back to their bad habits, placing the children in a precarious position of possible abuse, neglect and abandonment, again.

During the tweens and teens grandparents really need support in dealing with the multiple issues that face this age group today. Adolescence brings on a unique set of problems for each generation as the children grow and emotions run high. Children facing the reality that they have been abandoned by their parents, have witnessed physical, emotional, and drug abuse and lost their security are now faced with the typical problems of tweens and teens in the schools where they must find a way to be included or be faced with being placed in special education designation because schools do not have an area of expertise as to how to help these children. Many have been put into the position of fending for themselves in abusive households and now find society expecting them to relinquish that control while fears penetrate their very being.

Obtaining guardianship for these children is difficult and without guardianship, grandparents are at a loss in obtaining educational or medical help. There are programs being initiated in most states addressing this problem, but many times the guardianship is held up because of familial fights over who should have guardianship. The biggest problem with guardianship is that it is a temporary solution, leaving the high possibility of children being moved again. Since grandparents do not have legal standing in the court system, they are at the mercy of the system that is supposed to protect the children, many finding themselves financially and emotionally drained as the children are taken away without even allowing visitation with the grandparents who have loved and nurtured them. .

Legal assistance is available for low-income seniors where the children are already in the system, but others must pay lawyers out of their pockets to obtain the necessary legal status to properly care for the children. Pro Bono help is lacking in every State.

You saved me from the monsters!

Life goes on, the sun rises and sets
It pays no attention to the hurts and joys we encounter
It still rises and sets; it still maintains its' beauty
Our hopes are renewed with each day; worry and peace play in
our minds
Which will it be today? Life is changing and we must move on
Happier things are sure to come...BANG...life changes
The monsters in the closet have escaped and are attacking
Too little to fight, he needs help
"You saved me from the monsters!"
What job have I been given? No Joan of Arc am I!
How do I save the little babe? The monsters are threatening
I cannot ignore him...I must do something
Please God, a plan, a plan, I need help!

By Peggy O'Connor

Their Stories

These are just a few representative stories of grandmothers who are raising their grandchildren. There are millions more.

Please note that names and locations have been changed to protect the identities of the families.

One grandmother lives with her two grandchildren. She is divorced and had a lucrative career in sales where she received numerous awards. Active in civil and church groups, she had a busy life and a solid income. She had her own home and car. She raised two children, one is successfully employed, and studying law. The other is a drug addict who has had continuous problems throughout her life, mothered six children, none of which she was able to raise. All of the children have been raised in foster care or kinship care.

She now lives in low-income housing with rodent problems which are ignored by the management. Her car is now old and needs a great deal of upkeep. She depends on loans and gifts to keep the car going. She is involved in school and church with the children. Relatives, including her ex-husband provide her with some financial assistance. Local charitable groups help with food, furniture and other needed supplies. She is warmed by the love and care of the people who do this for her. It gives her courage to continue.

She attends college online and works part-time doing telephone work. She hopes to find a job that she can work during school hours to be there for her grandchildren. She has anticipated her upcoming 65th birthday knowing that now she would finally be insured by Medicare.

While these difficulties are there, she is quick to talk about the happy times she and her grandchildren have. They dream together of future good times where they would live in a nice house have a nice car and do fun things. Holidays are spent driving several hours to their great-grandparents home to help them out as they can no longer get out of the house. When asked if she would do things differently, she is quick to respond: "no way, I wish I had done it earlier"

A grandmother in another state is caring for her three minor grandchildren and her adult son who is a paraplegic. The grandmother herself is in ill health. They do not qualify for assistance so money is spread thin. Despite having her own health issues, she forgets her own pain and moves on; ignoring her own needs to meet the needs of the children, her grandchildren. She makes sure that the children go to school and church. She also assists her son in his care. This grandmother qualifies for no assistance from the state or federal government. Surely you would think that her problems are severe enough to qualify her for help. However, the reality is that her case is just not bad enough. There is always someone in worse circumstances, as hard as that is to realize. While her case is known in the system, there is no help. There is an unwritten rule that if someone is in more need; they get the help first, leaving nothing for struggling grandparents. Though her frustration is great, she feels she must go on for her son and her grandchildren.

Legal problems with the biological mother necessitate a lawyer to intervene and that is expensive. The mother of the children is a drug addict and has developed mental health issues from the drug abuse. She will not cooperate in relinquishing the custody of the children. The legal expenses involved in obtaining this precious custody of the children are too prohibitive to comprehend. Without the custody rights, this grandmother cannot obtain the help through the school district that her grandchildren need so desperately. The children have been damaged by the actions of the parent. Behavioral problems exist because the biological mother was on drugs during her pregnancies. Her obsession with her drug habit and the drugs passed on to the children during pregnancy has left their mark. How does this grandmother deal with that? There is no help with counseling that the children need so much. Will an occasional basket of poor quality food change this situation? Her only hope is that the laws will be changed to give grandparents more rights. While she waits for Federal and State programs to give cases like hers priority, she will give her grandchildren her unconditional love, but will this be enough to get them through the disastrous problems they have inherited? Probably not.

Another grandmother lives in the south where she recently moved to ensure her grandson the best education in a private school. She is easily engaged in conversation. She thanks God for her blessings. She's entering the teenage years again, for the 5th time. She's been there for them all, taking them into her home and her heart when needed. No questions, no conditions, no regrets.

Suffering through heart attack, cancer and mini strokes, she is a survivor. She goes on, maintaining a good home for her grandson against all odds. She attends church twice a week and thanks God she has survived and is able to care for her grandson. She teaches him to be thankful also. She spends little time thinking about her losses, including her husband who died within three weeks of diagnosis of prostrate cancer.

She is proud of her work ethics, her commitment, and her love. Her love is unconditional. It's her family....that's it. Everyone says she should write a book about all she has survived, but she accepts her story as similar to many others.

Watching the squirrels run up and down the trees in her yard, she plans trips to amusement parks and other places to create the memories so necessary for children to have. She will parent him, setting expectations and goals. She also will pay the majority of the costs of raising this teenager, as she has with the other four. No complaints. It would be nice to have help, but she understands. Showing the strength of so many Americans, she will survive!

In the Midwest, a 70 year old grandmother (you would never guess it) is raising her grandson. She is tall and thin and moves with grace. She has a professional aura about her and speaks with a soft voice and demeanor. You are confident she knows what she is talking about as she tells her story about her 13 year old grandson who is diagnosed as ADHD. His mother's live-in boyfriend cooked drugs in the kitchen microwave while his mother was pregnant. The effect was similar to second hand smoke. He was born 2 months prematurely at 3.5 lbs with fetal alcohol syndrome which left neurological damage, manifested in part by his ADHD. His lungs had not developed properly so he has many respiratory problems. She took over his care when he was 18 months old. Her daughter loves the child, but is ill equipped to make the right decisions for herself, let alone a child, which compromises his safety. As his advocate, she works with his school to meet his needs. She has him in a private school and structures his life balancing loving care and discipline. If he wants to play basketball on Saturday, he has to participate in Church on Sunday. She encourages appropriate relationships. Saturday morning finds his friends coming over for a special waffle breakfast. She then takes them skating or to the movies, always keeping them occupied.

She is quick to share many amusing stories of her childhood in an almost folksy way, emphasizing the simplicity of life for children in those days when she grew up in a large city with two brothers. She cannot understand why children are so angry today and it saddens her to see this anger. The increase in sexual activity at a young age, drugs, and body piercing are all of great concern to her. She strongly feels children need more education in these areas. She is concerned that there are many young parents who are ill equipped to parent their children because they are emotionally still children themselves. Divorced when her children were in grade school, she joined the foster care program and took in 20 children in five years. She worked in a program of emergency foster care where she took in children without notice, many suffering from serious emotional problems. Most were sexually active early in their teens. 90% of the children she took in were sexually abused. Most moved out of foster care by being legally emancipated at age 18 from parents or legal guardians and entered into the welfare system to afford them assistance in housing and childcare. You can hear the pain in her voice as she talks of these children. She frequently fought for these children because she saw that they were literally dumped into the system without any education in birth control, parenting or finances. She knows children. She ran a daycare out of her home for 23 years. She witnessed the behaviors of emotional and sexual abuse in the home. She feels badly that she could not help more. Though her life is full with responsibilities, she seeks out homeless people on the street and literally gives them the coat off her back, food and a few dollars. She knows that as they sleep in the shelters at night their coats get stolen. She doesn't ask why they are homeless. She just sees to their needs. Besides her three daughters, she had three foster girls that lived with her for 5/ 6 years. They remain like family and they and their children call her Nana. These children she was able to help.

When asked what she would like people to say about her when she is gone, she was quick to answer: "That I was there to help".

When asked what her dream is she stated: "If I had a good deal of money, I would open a home for wayward girls where they could be loved and taught the skills to survive in life". I asked her about "her" dreams. She admitted she would like to: "Retire in the Bahamas and live in the sun, on the water, around happy people." She also admitted that now that she is "getting younger" she would like to downsize to a two bedroom apartment where she can have an office to learn more about the computer she got six years ago and maybe will write her story. "I'm glad I'm as young as I am." She does not easily admit to the arthritis in her spine which causes her a good deal of pain.

As we closed the interview, she stated: "They're all our children, but the ones who have our blood are ours to be responsible for". It was difficult to follow my interview criteria because it was quickly apparent that this lady had so much to tell and even a two hour interview could not include everything. She laments that she misses social interaction that used to flow freely but has abated because of insecurities and lack of trust she feels have grown throughout the population.

One of her present concerns is that her grandson is turning 13 and talking about moving in with his mom and her boyfriend. She understands his desire to be with his mother, but is concerned that the structure she has maintained for him will be lost, putting him in danger of the many problems teens experience today.

Why do it? Why take on the tremendous task of raising a second family?

It was a cold and stormy night in January, 1990 when our first grandchild was born. A c-section was being performed in the hopes of saving mother and baby. Eight years previously, our daughter had gone through surgery, radiation and chemotherapy for a brain tumor. The fact that she was pregnant was a miracle in itself. The baby was 2lbs. 9oz.

Seeing the happiness on my daughter's face brought tears to my eyes. She so deserved to be happy, but happiness was not long lived when seven weeks later she was rushed back to the ER where they found the tumor had returned. "One in a hundred chances of living three days". The wind was knocked out of me. We had fought by her side to beat the tumor and we had won, but here we were facing it again. The baby was baptized at her bedside and she again went into surgery to remove a tumor. Only this time it was buying time, not a cure. After nine months of radical chemo, she died: her son was 14 months old. I have been asked why we decided to take in our grandson after our daughter's death. 18 years ago I would have answered: "he needs us...he is our daughter's child". Today my immediate response would still be: "he needs us". The bio dad came from a severely dysfunctional family who were clearly a danger to the child (history of seizure disorders, rape/incest, mental illness and genetic problems). Their ignorance of how to care for a child was phenomenal. Paternal grandmother had long history of bi-polar disorder and found dogs to be more important than humans, especially children (she fed our grandson dog food). The family history was well hidden until after the wedding. We knew they were weird but could not see the extent of the problems.

When our daughter died, how could we turn our backs on her child? He was born at 28 weeks at 2lbs9oz and came into our care at 4.5lbs. The bio dad was not capable to parent a child. Caring for an adult daughter in hospice and a premature newborn was certainly a challenge, but we survived. I lived my life reactively at that time and learned the true meaning of one day at a time.

Why did I do it? Would I make the same decision today? Of course! He's my grandchild and I would make the decision in a heartbeat! No regrets, no looking back. He's 19 now and still carries the baggage of abuse from the time he spent with bio dad and step mom. However, he is very much our son. We have a bond that cannot be broken. He is our son. I am his "grandmom".

The Problems

Studies have shown that children placed with family members over strangers do better. Children and Family Services now rely on grandparents to step in and care for the children. Dependent on variables like location, income, etc, CPS have begun programs to assist in adoption to give the grandchildren the needed stability to develop physically and emotionally. Biological parents are many times out of the picture as they battle their own demons of substance abuse or mental illness. Children come to grandparents suffering from ADD, ADHD, Crack Cocaine addiction (or brain damage from it), Post Traumatic Stress Disorder and Attachment Disorder. The developmental levels of growth are disturbed by abuse, neglect, and abandonment. Children do not develop the security of home and family that is necessary to develop a stable personality.

Laws work against grandparents and therefore courts do not recognize them. Many grandparents take in their grandchildren for many years and absorb the emotional, physical, and financial obligations of parenting, only to be called into court to forfeit the custody to the biological parent. Since grandparents do not have legal standing, they cannot fight to save the grandchildren who are faced with the emotional ups and downs of parental rights. While the courts are supposed to rule in the "best interest of the child", parental rights usually are stronger in affecting the outcome. The parents have the right to keep grandchildren away from the grandparents who have been in the parenting role, again putting the children into loss and confusion.

There is a wealth of information available on the Internet, offering any or all of these services. However, if they offer financial assistance, you better be living at or, below the poverty level. If you own a home, if you work, if you have a car or any other assets, you will not qualify. Politicians continue to okay entitlement programs for those living in poverty but the majority of families are considered middle class and do not qualify for the programs offered, even though their income may be obviously insufficient to support the grandparents and the grandchildren.

If purchasing a new home, generally, grandparents do not have the income to get approval for large mortgages. Rentals are restricted in number of children and sometimes just do not want children. It places grandparents in a precarious position of not being able to provide adequate housing for them and their grandchildren.

Behavior Problems:

Behavior problems in grandchildren are a problem for grandparents. Abuse, neglect, financial problems, and abandonment all play a role in the child's development, or lack thereof. Emotional problems born of this treatment enhances the need for identification of problems and appropriate treatment.

Many times, family and friends refuse support to grandparents who take in their grandchildren. Understanding why a grandparent would care so much seems to be lacking in many areas. Other children do not feel their parents should pay the price for sibling's failures, nor should they. Even if a grandparent has sufficient financial resources, friends who are planning long overdue vacations, concerns about savings and investments, and the right to privacy after raising their children, tend to exclude friends again back in the parenting role, who need the support. of friends and family.

Generally, schools do not have a category for this population. They assume parents will be involved and grandparents are only temporary caregivers. Increasingly, this is not the case. Grandparents must become involved in the curriculum the children must learn to give them continuity in their education. Teachers are at a loss in assisting grandparents in this challenge. In a University of Virginia Study on Grandparents Raising Grandchildren, it is pointed out that it is necessary for the grandparents to relearn parenting skills, acknowledging the challenges today in raising children, especially teenagers. However, programs offered in school districts are offered to the norm, not the individual.

School social workers, unless working in an inner city where poverty rates are high, are not knowledgeable of the resources available to families in need. School psychiatrists have different criteria in each state. In some states, they do not have to have a degree in psychology, nor do they have to have a doctorate degree. How can these people be expected come up with a plan for these children when they are not even equipped to diagnose the problem?

Grandparents are faced with schools that are not equipped to handle the unique challenges of these children. Poor performance and acting out behavior is considered the fault of the child, the parents or the grandparents. In most cases, the parents are not involved and the damage that has been done by neglect, abuse or abandonment have created a good majority of these children who suffer from Post Traumatic Stress Disorder, and/or Attachment Disorder. These are not conditions usually acknowledged by school districts, putting the children in a system that cannot offer them the help they need.

Private therapy is expensive and insurance covers a very small percentage, if any. Again, unless the grandparents are living in poverty, they do not qualify for assistance with therapy bills. Private therapy groups many times offer services on a sliding scale, but this too is another burden on the grandparents which they have not planned for. Private and/or community based therapy groups are stretched to the limits financially and cannot take on the task of dealing with these children, unless their behavior becomes a severe problem.

There is a book written by Dr. Bruce Perry, A Boy Who Was Raised as a Dog. It is about children who suffer traumatic experiences through abuse, neglect, natural disaster and accident. Dr. Perry discusses the changes in the development of these children and how it affects their growth. His work is very eye opening in what happens to children when they suffer through traumas. Now, if losing a parent, or parents, is not a trauma for a child, I clearly do not understand what is.

These children come to their grandparents seeking love and assurance. They go to school seeking caring teachers who might understand what they themselves cannot. Does their behavior show their needs? Probably not. They may very well be a behavior problem, acting out inappropriately and do poor work. They may be loud and obnoxious. I challenge any parent or teacher to read Dr. Perry's book and blame the child.

The question is often asked: "what happened...things weren't like this when I was a kid". No, they were not. The majority of today's grandparents were raised in a post war world with a high likelihood they lived in a home with a two parent family and siblings. You had your own possessions, like your bed, your toys, and your family. What would your life have been like if all of that was taken away from you? Stop and think. If you came home from school one day and found your parents were gone, who would you rely on? If you had to leave your home and go live somewhere else, what would happen to your things? Stop and think. Baseball cards, catcher's mitt, dolls and books, all yours, but now they may be gone.

I remember, as a child, living in a very big home with extended family surrounding me and neighbors who were there for any child in need. My mom insisted we take afternoon naps. One Sunday afternoon in the summer of my sixth year, I awakened to a quiet room with breezes silently wafting through the open window, moving the sheer curtains like miniature ghosts flying in. I crept out of bed and slowly took the grand staircase, one at a time, listening for my mother's voice, wishing her to walk out and greet me. I was fearful of the silence that surrounded me. Upon reaching the bottom of the stairs, the fear grew to acknowledging that no one was there. They must have left while I slept! As I tiptoed through the living room and dining room, my hearing became aware of every whisper, of every breath of air that filled the room, in anticipation of finding my mother. As I approached the kitchen, I heard the whoosh of the kitchen faucet and the sound of pans clinking on the sink top. I cautiously turned the corner to see my mother working quietly at the sink, preparing our dinner. I don't think she ever knew my great sense of relief when I saw her. It was enough to hear her words as she asked if I had a good nap. Relief consumed me as I hugged her and went to play, finding my sister and friends playing quietly in the grass.

Many years later, when my mother was in the nursing home with Alzheimer's, I entered her room with the same trepidation I had in childhood, wondering if she was there, if she was okay. The days before she died left me empty with loss as I observed her in a semi fetal position in the bed, not knowing whether she knew I was there or not. I would ask her if she had a nice nap......only to receive the blank stare emanating from her fevered eyes. Somehow though I knew that by holding her hand, she knew I was there, as she had been for me so many years ago.

"Kids just show no respect anymore."

It's true. Today's teenager, in general, does not show respect. You might get some that will say please and thank you, or hold the door for you, but they generally do not show respect. The question remains as to why they do not. I pose the question: "Why should they?" As grandparents, we come from a generation that highly respected the elderly, with grandparents living in the home in many cases. But, have you asked yourself the question of who taught them to show respect? Yes, I know you will say that you disciplined your children and they know consequences. But home is not the only place they learn respect.

In the past ten years, we have had a steady onslaught of shocking occurrences. Sports figures are arrested for abusing women and animals. I heard a report on a famous golfer who has recently been in the news for cheating on his wife numerous times with numerous women. He professed his apologies to his family and the public for his actions. The reporters and fans who were calling in were of the opinion that the golfer was, after all, a good looking young man with billions of dollars, which made him a prime target for beautiful women to pursue him.

The bottom line was that the poor guy was human and would be expected to fall prey to these women, thereby excusing him for breaking the commitment to his wife and family. After all, the "guy is only human". Religious leaders have been sued for sexual abuse of minors, and secret homosexual affairs while married. Politicians have openly admitted discretions. Of course, as each one was accused, they lied on national TV that they were not guilty, until the facts came out. Policemen have been fired for abusing prisoners. Babysitters abuse the children in their care. Teachers are now unionized and profess that it is not their job to take care of problem children. School administrators are paid huge salaries and given luxurious benefits to build our educational system. Court battles are fought over who "deserves" to have custody of the children. All of this is brought to our attention on national TV every hour on the half hour.

The courts protect the rights of the biological parent over the rights of the child, even if they are not meeting the needs of their children, Drug abuse, mental illness and lack of responsibility are accepted by the courts who do not find many of these parents unfit.

Children are not blind or deaf to the stories of personalities. They hear us talking, they hear the TV. They experience some themselves in their daily lives. So who has taught them to respect? Abuse of the elderly is on the rise by 10/18 year old kids. Teachers are having love affairs with their students.

There is only one area that children can look up to: Rock Stars. Now before you tell me this is ridiculous, let me point something out. Rock Stars are consistent. They don't change and they accept. This brings a false sense of structure to kids, especially teenagers. They make a lot of money and live lives full of luxury. They also use drugs and alcohol in extreme. But they are not pushing the kids away. They are not letting them down (at least in the child's eyes). Why wouldn't kids look up to them? The very basics of our society have let them down. The question I have to ask is: "Who is teaching the children respect?"

Kids Adjust

Kids adjust, or so they say
They forget…go on and play
Kids adjust to being ignored
Kids adjust to emotional abuse
Kids adjust to physical abuse
Kids will still play
Kids will still laugh
The play will be different
The laugh will be strained
In their eyes you will see the story told
Kids adjust, or so they say
But HOW do they adjust?

Schools do not easily accept the diagnosis of outside professionals, many thinking if there is a problem, children should be placed in special classes, special schools, put on medication or place the burden on the grandparents to prepare the child at home to fit into the "norm" when they attend school. I doubt this is out of maliciousness, but they just don't know what to do. They don't have training, a diagnosis, or aids in how to help these children.

Many of the children suffer from Attachment Disorder because of the many losses they have suffered in their young lives. This is a serious diagnosis which requires qualified treatment. I again refer to Dr. Bruce Perry's book: "The Boy Who Was Raised as a Dog", where he relates what happens especially after the children are sent to a professional, like him. I highly recommend this book if one wants to understand what happens to many children, through no fault of their own.

Teachers and other school personnel do not fully understand what effect their actions, or lack of actions, have on the children in their care. Teacher unions are quick to state that if children have significant problems the teachers should not be responsible for their care. But if we do not learn to work together to help the children, our society is doomed.

If at least 80% of the children in this group are coming from parents with drug/alcohol abuse problems, you can be guaranteed that many were born with Fetal Alcohol Syndrome, Crack Cocaine withdrawal, and many with brain damage from this abuse. They start out in life fighting the odds. Yet, when they get to school, it is too much trouble to find a way to work with them. When they get to the teen years, many have already been labeled and their self esteem is destroyed. Many get into serious trouble and wind up incarcerated or on drugs, like their parents. Is there nothing we can do to stop this trend?

What is a grandparent's responsibility in their grandchild's education?

Times do change and teaching our grandchildren the way it used to be done is no longer adequate. As grandparents taking in our grandchildren, we can expect at least one to need Special Education. Answers do not always come easily as the problem precipitating the failure to thrive in a school environment is unknown. Until now, there were two types of placements in schools: special Ed and regular. Educators have known for several years that many children are falling through the cracks and not succeeding in school. It is no wonder that the number of high school drop outs has increased tremendously over the past 10 years.

One rule that must be followed is that children do want to learn. If they are not learning, we need to look to the educators and speak up as we are the child's advocate. If you have a grandchild who is struggling, consider the following because. Education is finally coming up with a possible answer. A new approach is the following:

Response to Intervention (RTI)

By Susan Bruce, Regional Education Coordinator (RTI)

A Parent Guide to RTI was created by Susan Bruce, Regional Education Coordinator for PRO*Parents of South Carolina, Inc. The Guide explains the RTI process and what IDEA requires, parent concerns and important questions about RTI, and what RTI means for our kids.

What is RTI?

RTI is a tiered process of instruction that allows schools to identify struggling students early and provide appropriate instructional interventions. Early intervention means more chances for success and less need for special education services. RTI would also address the needs of children who previously did not qualify for special education.

What RTI is NOT
  Special seating in classroom
  Shortened assignments
  Parent-teacher conferences
  Suspension
  Retention
  "More of the same" general classroom instruction

The purpose of RTI is to:
  catch struggling children early
  provide appropriate instruction
  prevent the need to refer the child for special education. Early intervention means more chances for success and less need for special education services. RTI would also address the needs of children who previously did not qualify for special education.

In an attempt by the US Department of Education to eliminate the wall that separates regular and special education, school districts may use 15% of IDEA funding for early intervention services in regular education—RTI.

If you want more information on this subject go to: www.wrightslaw.com and read their full newsletter report.

When A Teacher Makes A Difference.

My daughter followed her love for dance and earned a Bachelor Degree in Fine Arts for Dance. Though she had the opportunity to perform, she chose to teach. She now is married with children of her own but still teaches. She loves the kids she teaches and is many times brought to tears worrying about something going wrong in one of their lives. Each year as students move on to college and pursuing their careers, she sheds her tears and wishes them well.

Too few times in life we receive recollection or thanks for what we do. We certainly all receive criticism but always wonder if we are getting through to the chorus. Recently my daughter received a note from a former student who is unnamed...

"Tonight I went to my little cousin's Dance Competition. Throughout the evening I kept thinking how wonderful it would be to see you again. I want you to know, that you were a big part of my life as a youngster. The first time I ever saw you dance (It Had to Be You), I thought you were the most beautiful woman. You are so talented.

I'm sure you heard about dad, he passed away a couple of years ago and throughout that time I have been flooded with memories. Dance has been a part of all the good things I remember in my life. There were bad times, but for some reason I can't recall those memories.

There have been very few people that loved and protected me like you did. When I was with you I felt safe. Many times I felt like I was trapped in a world that would never know how scared I was inside, but every so often we would have a talk and I would realize that I was going to be ok.

It is interesting to hear my brother and sister talk about their person that was there for them when dad got sick. You were my person. You were the one that turned on the music and let me dance my pain away. You were the one that challenged me enough to keep my mind sharp. You were the one who ran for me when I split to bathroom to cry. I never forget you. I now work with children of all ages. Some of them have had worse things happen and have had no one to turn to for help. I was so fortunate to have such a wonderful role model like you. I don't physically dance anymore, but I move gracefully throughout life. I am passionate in my job. I have this innate ability to flow and connect with others. I dance through life. I guess what I am trying to say is thank you. I needed you. Even when I was in high school and we didn't have as much time together, you still looked out for me. Thank you. You will always have a special place in my heart. You taught me so much more than how to dance.

Love always."

The Answers

Failure to Thrive, ADD, ADHD, Attachment Disorder, Post Traumatic Stress Disorder. These are diagnosis being used on children today, children who do not "fit" into the norm. In Dr. Perry refers to the vulnerability of children to stress and trauma, and the effect it has on their brain development.

It is easy to note the serious cases of abuse and neglect. We all are amazed at these cases and utter statements like: "How could anyone do that to a child?" The unfortunate reality is that children are going through stress and traumas every day, in every neighborhood. The children are marked by theses experiences, for life. Yet, society labels them as ADD, ADHD, Behavior Disordered, and educators tend to blame the home life of the child.

When we were little, my sister and I played with dolls, hugging them, cleaning them, feeding them, and talking to them. Why did we partake in this play? We were imitating the adults around us. As babies, we were held, cleaned, fed, and spoken to. We responded to these adults who cared for us and in turn, started early to exercise this interaction with dolls and then our children. Now I can't say that my mother was the biggest cuddlier, but she cared for everybody in her life, daily meeting the needs of others. However, I also had my grandmother living in our house, who worked in a factory all day. When she came home, she was all ours, mine especially. We had a big ole rocking chair, just large enough to hold a chubby grandma and grandchild. After about 20 minutes of rocking and cuddling with Gram, the world was a wonderful place. As I grew into adulthood, I vowed my children would receive that same loving care. The rocking chair was a must before the birth of my first child. I had three children and they each were rocked to sleep in my arms every night, without fail. If they fell down, they were rocked and soothed. When my grandson came home at 4.5 lbs, he was held and rocked. My daughter has had two children and they too, have been rocked and held. As Gram grew older, she rocked her days away. As her hands lay on the arms of the chair, her fingers gently mimicked the rocking motion, stroking the wood of the chair. Just watching her do this, brought back good feelings to me. She held court in that chair as we grew older and seemed to have an unending list of solutions to our problems, though basically, it always came down to: accept life, trust in God, and do you best. She somehow knew we would survive whatever came our way. She was right. I have survived.

Kids and Stress

kidshealth.org/ teen/ your_mind/ emotions/ stress.html
One cannot dismiss the fact that children who have been abused, neglected and abandoned by their parents are prime candidates for a diagnosis of stress. Anxiety exists over not knowing where you will be living, where your belongings are, who will care for you and simply: "Who will be there when I get home from school?"

According to kidshealth.org there are two kinds of stress: good and bad. They state:

The stress response (also called the fight or flight response) is critical during emergency situations, such as when a driver has to slam on the brakes to avoid an accident. It can also be activated in a milder form at a time when the pressure's on but there's no actual danger — like stepping up to take the foul shot that could win the game, getting ready to go to a big dance, or sitting down for a final exam. A little of this stress can help keep you on your toes, ready to rise to a challenge. And the nervous system quickly returns to its normal state, standing by to respond again when needed.

But stress doesn't always happen in response to things that are immediate or that are over quickly. Ongoing or long-term events, like coping with a divorce or moving to a new neighborhood or school, can cause stress, too.

Long-term stressful situations can produce a lasting, low-level stress that's hard on people. The nervous system senses continued pressure and may remain slightly activated and continue to pump out extra stress hormones over an extended period. This can wear out the body's reserves, leave a person feeling depleted or overwhelmed, weaken the body's immune system, and cause other problems.

What Are the Symptoms of PTSD (Post Traumatic Stress Disorder)?

Whether it occurs right after the trauma or later on, PTSD has certain characteristic symptoms that usually develop within 3 months of the traumatic event. People generally experience some or all of these symptoms:

reliving the traumatic event. Many people with PTSD have nightmares, flashbacks, or disturbing mental images about the trauma.

avoiding reminders of the trauma. People with PTSD may avoid people, places, or activities that remind them of the stressful event. They may also avoid talking about what happened.

emotional numbness. Many people with PTSD feel numb or detached; they may not feel same as before or the same way about other people or the world. This could be caused by the overproduction of certain chemicals that block sensation during extreme stress.

hypervigilance. People with PTSD may be easily startled, on edge, jumpy, irritable, or tense. This may be due to high levels of stress hormones in the body. Difficulty concentrating and trouble sleeping may also be part of this hyper-alert state.

They go on to discuss who develops PTSD:

People of any age — kids, teens, and adults — can develop PTSD. But not everyone who experiences a serious trauma develops it. In fact, most people do not. Many recover from life-threatening traumas (after a normal reaction to the stressful event and the right support) without having a lasting problem. This ability to cope and bounce back is called resilience.

The intensity or circumstances of a trauma can influence a person's vulnerability to PTSD, too. National disasters like the terrorist attacks of 9/11 or the 2007 shooting at Virginia Tech can cause widespread anxiety, regardless of whether the person was there or not. In some cases, seeing these events and the traumatic images portrayed on TV and the Internet can lead to symptoms of PTSD.

Housing

Housing is a problem because many grandparents have downsized to smaller living quarters and bringing in grandchildren increases the necessarily to move to a larger home. Grandparents who live in senior communities are forced to leave because of no-children clauses. Grandparents find themselves looking for a home with enough space for growing children, good school districts, and safe neighborhoods. A retirement budget does not cover these expenses.

In Chicago IL there is a new concept in housing being tried: Sankofa Safe Child Initiative

The mission of Sankofa is to keep families intact. Its vision is to refer families to specific community resources, churches, social service agencies and health providers that can give meaningful, effective solutions to their urgent needs. Sankofa partnered with and houses the Community Coordinating Council for Juvenile Justice. The goal of the Juvenile Justice Initiative is to develop a local governance structure to bring together systems and community stakeholders to design, implement, and operate an integrated continuum of community-based systems that will work to reduce the numbers of youth in the juvenile system and improve the lives of vulnerable youth. Sankofa will continue to work with the Community Justice for Youth Institute (CJYI) to further the development of the Community Coordinating Council as a mechanism for collaboration among community and system stakeholders. Sankofa will facilitate the collaboration of grassroots community and juvenile justice stakeholders, to develop effective local governance mechanisms to coordinate and promote an appropriate, sustainable, continuum of restorative, community-based sanctions and services for youth. Residents of this housing are a combination of grandparents raising grandchildren and kinship care families who reside along with young singles who are transitioning from foster care to independence. Social workers are available to ease problems. Caseworkers keep tabs progress and are able to offer assistance where needed.

The Bronx, New York

A new apartment complex in the Bronx, New York, houses a unique clientele of grandparents raising their grandchildren. In most cases, grandparents obtained custody of their grandchildren because the children's parents died, were incarcerated, or had their parental rights terminated because of substance abuse, mental illness, or child neglect. Grandparents stepped in to take care of the children, even though many did not have the financial capacity to do so. The 50 apartments in the GrandParent Family Apartments offer an affordable housing option to these low-income grandparents. They also offer a variety of services designed especially for this population and its wide age range. For instance, grandparents have access to a social worker, support groups, and parenting classes. Children can receive tutoring and take part in social events. Group meals are often made available for everyone. The project is the result of a public-private collaboration among three groups:

Presbyterian Senior Services sponsored the project, receiving money from low-income housing programs to produce equity for funding; they also provide the onsite services to residents. West Side Federation for Senior and Supportive Housing served as the developer. New York City Housing Authority donated the land and rental subsidies. Local, State, Federal, and private funds contributed to the project.

Studies

http://gerontologist.gerontologyjournals.org/cgi/content/abstract/45/2/262

Bert Hayslip, Jr., PhD1 and Patricia L. Kaminski, PhD1 (Study on Grandparents Raising Grandchildren)

An increasingly prevalent family constellation is a home headed by a grandparent who is raising grandchildren. We explore the state of our knowledge about such grandparents with particular attention to its implications for service providers and researchers. In our review we address several key areas: (a) the costs and benefits of raising a grandchild; (b) the heterogeneity of custodial grandparent caregivers; (c) the critical need for social support among custodial grandparents; (d) parenting practices and attitudes among grandparents raising grandchildren; and (e) helping efforts at multiple levels with custodial grandparents. We also discuss directions for research and practice concerning custodial grandparents.

Study from West Virginia University (C. Sue Miller, PHd http://www.wvu.edu/~exten/infores/pubs/fypubs/240.wlg.pdf) states behaviors of grandchildren being raised by grandparents. "Grandchildren who are too young to talk about their feelings or who simply can't verbalize what is going on in their heads usually act out these feelings in some way. Clinging, baby-like behavior, "testing" and "manipulating" behavior, eating, and sleeping disorders, and other symptoms may suggest extra reassurance is needed."

Grandparents who take in their grandchildren are not there to spoil them, or buy them presents. They are suddenly there to care for them, protect them, provide for them, and parent them. When we first took in our grandson we realized the job we had ahead of us. We had successfully raised three children. We knew what we were doing. But the big acknowledgement was that times had changed. Anyone who thinks that child rearing is the same, no matter the age of the parent, has their head stuck in the sand. We made a conscious decision early on not just to raise him, but to parent him. After making that decision, we ensued on a journey of learning how to raise a child in today's world. I am here to tell you that it is very different from times when we raised our children. It is ever so important to show structure in your life and in your home. You need to be ever observant to what the children are being exposed to. When we were younger, when our children were younger, hearing of a terrible crime was something that happened elsewhere and happened to someone else.

Today, we have lists of child sex abusers who may live next door, or down the block. We have teachers, priests, and scout leaders accused of abuse. It is of utmost importance to keep in tune with the children. You have to be more liberal in understanding the music they want to listen to, the friends they want to be with. My son has a friend who has long hair, wears stovepipe pants and a long black coat. By appearances you would say: "oh this kid is trouble". Actually, he is one of the most responsible kids I have met. I do not judge him by his looks, but by his behavior and he is always polite, soft spoken, and respectful. He is the one who offers to help clean up and always says good-by and thank you when he is leaving. I cannot say the same for some of the kids who come well dressed with expensive haircuts and popularity. They are the ones I watch. They may very well be the drug dealers of today.

http://www.uwex.edu/relationships/files/B3786-2.pdf
The Importance of Close Relationships
"What is attachment? Attachments are relationships that children form with the most special and trustworthy people in their lives. Although these relationships usually begin between infants and their parents at birth, attachments can form when children are older, too. The most common attachment is between mother and baby. However, the child could form an attachment with any person, including grandparents, aunts and uncles, older sibling, or babysitter) if the right type of care is given. By the time babies are 18 months old, they usually have formed attachment relationships with a few special people. In many families, these people are grandparents who are raising their grandchildren."
"These early attachment relationships are important for a child's social and emotional development. Having an adult in their lives who gives them emotional and physical support helps the child develop a sense of security, comfort and confidence. If there is no adult whom the child can count on, he or she may grow up not trusting in others."

Another study addresses children losing those close to them, the people they depend on:
Coping With Parental Loss Due to Termination of Parental Rights www.cwla.org

This article addresses the process by which children and adolescents cope with severe acute stress of parental loss from causes other than divorce or death. Participants were 60 children and adolescents from a residential treatment facility. Most had experienced neglect, physical abuse, and sexual abuse, and their parents had their parental rights terminated. Measures of symptomatology indicated that children reported low levels of depressive symptoms, whereas caregivers reported the children were experiencing significant psychological problems. Children used avoidant coping strategies more often than emotion-focused coping strategies, which, in turn, were used more than problem-focused coping strategies. Results are discussed in terms of helping children cope with parental loss.

"Children and adolescents who lose their parents because of a termination of parental rights (TPR) may respond with a variety of coping strategies, some of which may not promote good mental health. Despite their parents' maltreatment, these children often grieve the parental loss and may need specific help in developing coping strategies that help them heal and move forward."

"To study coping strategies, researchers interviewed 60 children and adolescents, ages 9-18, who had been removed from their parents because of abuse or neglect. After an average of eight placements in foster care, these children had been placed in residential treatment because of moderate to severe emotional difficulties."

"The researchers found that the children tended to use avoidant coping strategies the most, followed by emotion-focused coping strategies and problem-focused coping strategies. Only emotion-focused coping strategies, which involved focusing on feelings by expressing them, were associated with greater psychological symptomatology."

"Mental health practitioners who treat children grieving the loss of their parents due to TPR may want to shift their focus away from the expression of emotions to a more concrete focus that includes:"

Answering children's questions about the situation

Helping the children develop problem-solving skills

Working toward increasing self-esteem

Developing the children's interpersonal skills

Increasing the children's social network

This study, "Coping with Parental Loss Because of Termination of Parental Rights," by K. M. Schneider and V. Phares, was published in the November/December 2005 issue of *Child Welfare*. It is available through the Child Welfare League of America:

The Vera Institute of Justice conducted a study on children and grieving and issued the following statement: study can be found at:

http://www.vera.org/content/childhood-loss-and-behavioral-problems

Childhood loss and behavioral problems

"A growing body of evidence suggests that schools and other child-serving systems can help young people with behavioral problems by asking whether they have lost someone they love and responding constructively when answers suggest a child is grieving. Such actions could influence whether a child's behavioral problems spiral into ever wider levels of misbehavior or subside with appropriate help in confronting the challenges of their loss. In 2003, staff at the Vera Institute of Justice began working with a small number of intermediate and elementary schools in New York City to explore the links between loss and student misbehavior. Vera's goal was to identify students who had lost a loved one and develop therapeutic responses to help them. This report, which draws upon existing research, promising practices, and the experience of Vera personnel, is designed to increase policymakers' and practitioners' awareness of how the loss of a loved one influences children's behavioral problems. It also offers suggestions on how to identify grieving children and intervene in cycles of misbehavior tied to grief."

Where do grandparents stand legally?
http://www.ehow.com/about_5384528_custody-laws-grandparents.html

History
"Before 2000, grandparents could be granted court-ordered visitation with their grandchildren as long as the visitation was demonstrated to be in the best interests of the child. In Troxel v. Graville, the Supreme Court in 2000 invalidated a Washington state law that permitted "any person" to petition for visitation at "any time" when it was in the best interest of the child. The law was struck down because 1) it did not provide a presumption that fit parents act in the best interests of their children, 2) it failed to accord a fit parent's decision any special weight in the decision, and 3) it failed to place the burden on the person seeking visitation, rather than on the parents. "

States Respond
"Following Troxel v. Granville, state supreme courts nationwide retroactively struck down their own grandparent visitation laws, not only making it more difficult for grandparents to gain legal visitation but also invalidating any existing visitation

orders. Many grandparents cannot even seek relief from the courts to allow them to know their grandchildren. Following is a state by state summary of the laws affecting this population: If grandparents cannot appeal for visitation, the custody issue, when needed, is generally abandoned by the courts unless the children have made their way into the system and children and family services may help grandparents in custody issues."

http://grandparents.about.com/od/grandparentsrights/qt/

Alabama:

Grandparents visitation rights in the state of Alabama depend upon the family situation of the grandchild and a determination of the child's best interest. In order to qualify for a legal hearing, one of the following situations must exist:

The parents are divorced

A parent or parent is deceased

The child was born out of wedlock

The child was abandoned by a parent

The grandparents have been denied visitation.

Factors which the court may consider when determining the best interest of the child include the following:

The willingness of the grandparents to promote the relationship between the grandchild and his or her parents

The preference of the child

The mental and physical health of the child

The mental and physical health of the grandparents

Any evidence of domestic violence in the home

The wishes of the parents.

Adoption terminates grandparents visitation rights

Alaska

When rendering a judgment, the court will consider whether visiting with the grandparent is in the best interest of the child and whether the grandparent has established ongoing contact with the child or has tried to establish ongoing contact with the child. When determining whether to grant visitation and the terms of any visitation granted, the court is directed to consider whether there is a history of child abuse or domestic violence attributable to the grandparent's son or daughter, the parent of the grandchild.

If a grandparent wishes to request visitation with a child, and there has been no custody case, the grandparent will need the advice of an attorney.

Adoption terminates visitation rights unless the adoption decree specifies visitation rights for the child's natural relatives.

Arizona

Arizona is unusual in that it is specifically grants great-grandparents the same rights as grandparents. Those rights are, however, fairly rigidly defined. One of these conditions must be met: the marriage of the parents of the child must have been dissolved for at least three months, a parent must be deceased, a parent must have been officially declared missing for at least three months or the child must have been born out of wedlock. As in all states, the court must determine the best interest of the child, considering such issues as any historical relationship between the grandparent and child, the motivation of the person requesting visitation, the motivation of the person denying visitation, the quantity of time requested and the possible adverse impact that visitation will have on the child's customary activities. In addition, in the case of the death of a parent, the court may consider the benefits of maintaining a relationship with the extended family. Petitions for visitation rights can be filed as part of divorce or paternity proceedings, if either is held. Otherwise, the grandparents can petition the court separately for visitation.

Adoption terminates visitation rights unless the adopting party is a stepparent.

Arkansas

Arkansas specifically grants great-grandparents the same rights as grandparents. Grandparents or great-grandparents may request visitation rights if the parents' marital relationship has been severed by death, divorce, or legal separation. In addition, visitation may be requested if the child is in the custody or under the guardianship of a person other than a natural or adoptive parent, or if the child is illegitimate. In the case of an illegitimate child, a paternal grandparent may request visitation only if paternity has been established in court.

As in all of the United States, the court must decide that a visitation order would be in the best interest and welfare of the child. If a parent or guardian has denied visitation as not being in the best interest of the child, the grandparent seeking visitation must rebut that presumption. The grandparent must document a "significant and viable" relationship with the child. Such a relationship is presumed to have existed if the child resided with the grandparent for six or more months, the grandparent was the caregiver for six or more months or the grandparent had "frequent or regular" contact with the child for twelve or more months. The grandparent may offer other evidence that the loss of the relationship with the grandparent is likely to harm the child. Adoption terminates the visitation rights of the natural grandparents.

See the Arkansas statutes about grandparent visitation when the grandchild is in the custody of a parent and when the grandchild is not in the custody of a parent.

California

California grandparents cannot file for visitation rights while the child's parents are married, unless specific conditions are met. These conditions include the following: the parents are living separately, a parent's whereabouts are unknown for a month or more, the child has been adopted by a stepparent or the child does not live with either parent. In addition, a grandparent may petition for rights if joined in that petition by one of the parents.

Visitation rights are based on a pre-existing relationship that has "engendered a bond." The court is also directed to balance the interest of the child with the parents' rights and authority to make decisions about the child.

In 2007 the California laws were amended so that grandparents do not lose their rights if a stepparent adopts their grandchild.

Colorado

Colorado grandparents can file for visitation rights if the grandchild's parents are divorced or legally separated, if the child is in the custody of someone other than a parent or if the grandparent's child, who is the parent of the child, has died. If a parent loses his or her parental rights, the rights of his or her parents, the child's grandparents, are lost also.

In Colorado, parents who have denied visitation from grandparents are presumed to have acted in the child's best interest. This is, however, a "reputable presumption," meaning that grandparents can present evidence to the contrary. Grandparents must present "clear and convincing evidence" that either the parent is not fit to make this presumption or that the decision barring visitation is not in the best interests of the child. If the court orders visitation, it must cite the "special factors" on which it relied for its decision. The court may hold a hearing to make its determination or rely on the evidence presented in affidavits. A hearing is required if the custodial parent so requests.

Adoption terminates the visitation rights of grandparents unless the adopting party is a stepparent.

Connecticut

Connecticut statutes about child visitation have been amended so that they no longer specifically mention grandparents but say that visitation can be granted to "any person." The standards for "any person" receiving visitation rights in Connecticut have been set quite high.

First, most Connecticut grandparents cannot file for visitation rights on their own. They may only become a party in a court action brought by their child. Only grandparents who have filled the parental role with a child have the right to petition for visitation on their own, and they must contend that denying them access would cause "actual, significant harm." Thus Connecticut law sets a higher standard than the required consideration of the best interests of the child. In addition, the evidence offered must be "clear and convincing," which is also a higher standard than is often required in non-criminal cases.

Connecticut is also one of the minority of states in which adoption does not automatically cancel

Delaware

Delaware statutes allow grandparents "reasonable visitation rights" as determined by the court. However, when the parents of the child have an intact marriage and object to grandparent visitation, the court is unlikely to grant visitation in opposition to the parental wishes. The best interest of the child is, of course, always considered. The court may consider such factors as the wishes of the child and the nature of any prior relationship with the grandparent when determining the child's best interests. Delaware law further provides that if workable, the maternal grandparents should visit when the child is with the mother and the paternal grandparents when the child is with the father.

Adoption cuts off all visitation rights of grandparents.

Florida

The Florida Supreme Court has declared unconstitutional certain portions of the Florida statutes governing grandparent visitation. In the first finding, Beagle v. Beagle, the court decided that an intact family has the right to bar visits from grandparents. The second case, Von Eiff v. Azicri, involved a case in which a parent was deceased, but the surviving parent had remarried and had stopped the grandparents of the deceased from visiting. The court decided that the surviving parent had created an intact family, which then had the right to make that decision.

Three other court decisions have chipped away at the grandparent visitation statutes, but those statutes remain on the books because the Florida legislature has not removed them, nor have they enacted new laws. Opinions are divided about the validity of the Florida statutes in the wake of these Florida Supreme Court decisions. It is best to regard all statutes regarding grandparent visitation as unreliable until the Florida Legislature adopts new statutes. Grandparents seeking visitation rights in Florida must certainly seek the advice of a lawyer before deciding whether to proceed with a petition.

The existing statutes, whether applicable or not, instruct the courts to consider a lengthy list of factors in determining the best interests of the child. These factors include the willingness of the grandparent or grandparents to encourage a close relationship between the child and the parent or parents, the length and quality of the prior relationship between the child and the grandparent, the child's preference when he or she is old enough to express it, the mental and physical health of the child, the mental and physical health of the grandparent or grandparents and any other relevant factors. Great-grandparents are considered to have the same rights as grandparents. Adoption terminates grandparent visitation rights unless a stepparent adopts the child.

Georgia

In regard to adoption by a blood relative, Georgia Code states the following: "A grandparent with visitation rights to a child granted pursuant to Code Section 19-7-3 shall have the privilege to file objections to the petition of adoption if neither parent has any further rights to the child and if the petition for adoption has been filed by a blood relative of the child."

With the state of grandparent visitation thus in doubt in Georgia, grandparents seeking visitation will definitely need the services of an attorney.

Hawaii

In the state of Hawaii, grandparents may petition for visitation as long as the child's home state is Hawaii. Grandparent visitation in Hawaii has been impacted by a 2007 decision by the Hawaii Supreme Court which stated that the state's lower courts must adopt a test of whether upholding the parent's wishes could cause "harm" to the child, rather than the less stringent requirement of considering the best interest of the child. The court used Troxel v. Granville, the decision by the U.S. Supreme Court, as the basis of its decision. Hawaii thus joins Florida as one of the states in which the legislatures need to pass new statutes about grandparent visitation as the result of state Supreme Court rulings

Idaho

The state statutes of Idaho contain a single sentence about grandparent visitation rights. "The district court may grant reasonable visitation rights to grandparents or great-grandparents upon a proper showing that the visitation would be in the best interests of the child."

In 2009 the Idaho State Senate proposed a more detailed draft of grandparent visitation rights, Senate Bill 1105. The bill died at the end of the legislative session.

Illinois

Following the U.S. Supreme Court case of Troxel v. Granville, the Illinois state statutes concerning grandparent visitation rights were declared unconstitutional by the Illinois Supreme Court. Following legislation passed in 2005 and 2007, grandparents once more have legal rights to visitation under certain circumstances. These circumstances include parents not living with one another, an absent parent, a deceased parent or a parent joining the grandparent's petition. In the case of a child born out of wedlock, paternity must be established before the paternal grandparents may be allowed visitation. Visitation is also not allowed if the parents surrender the child to any party other than a foster care service or the Illinois Department of Children and Family Services. To bring the Illinois statutes in line with Troxel v. Granville, the law includes a provision that the burden is on the grandparent or other petitioner to prove that the parent's decision to bar visitation is harmful to the child's mental, physical, or emotional health.

The Illinois statutes also apply to great-grandparents and siblings. Adoption cuts off the legal rights of the grandparents unless the adoption is by a stepparent.

The Illinois statutes are quite long and complex and contain several other stipulations. See Illinois statutes.

Indiana

In the state of Indiana, grandparents may request visitation in the case of a deceased parent, a marriage terminated in Indiana or a child born out of wedlock. Marriages terminated outside of Indiana must meet a different set of standards. In the case of a child born out of wedlock, paternity must have been established in order for paternal grandparents to file a petition.

As in all states, grandparents must show that visitation is in the child's best interest. The child may be interviewed in chambers in order to make this determination. In addition, grandparents must demonstrate "meaningful contact" with the grandchild or attempts to establish "meaningful contact."

Adoption cuts off the legal rights of the grandparents unless the adoption is by a stepparent, natural grandparent, sibling, aunt, uncle, niece or nephew.

Iowa

In 2001 and 2003 the Iowa Supreme Court struck down portions of the grandparent visitation statutes. In 2007 the legislature passed new statutes. Under the new law, grandparents must "clearly and convincingly" prove that they have a substantial relationship with the grandchild, that the custodial parent is unfit to make a decision about visitation and that visitation is in the best interest of the child. Great-grandparents have the same rights as grandparents. Since the law has been in effect only for a short time, it is not firmly established what types of proof are necessary to prove the preceding conditions.

Kansas

In the state of Kansas, visitation rights are awarded in custody orders. Adoption ends visitation rights unless the grandparent's child who is the parent is deceased and the stepparent adopts the child. Prior relationship between the grandparent and grandchild is considered when awarding visitation rights.

Kentucky

In Kentucky, "reasonable visitation rights" may be awarded to either paternal or maternal grandparents if the court determines that it is in the best interest of the child to do so. These visitation rights may even survive the termination of parental rights belonging to the grandparent's son or daughter, who is the father or mother of the child, if the court decides that visitation is in the child's best interest.

A grandparent whose child is deceased and who supplies child support for a grandchild can be awarded visitation rights that are the equivalent of a non-custodial parent's. Grandparents rights granted under this condition will not be terminated even if the parental rights of the grandparent's son or daughter are terminated.

Adoption ends grandparent visitation rights unless the adopting party is the stepparent and the grandparent's child has not suffered termination of parental rights.

Louisiana

Three statutes govern visitation rights in Louisiana, making it one of the trickier systems to navigate. In the statute which applies to the majority of cases, grandparents may be awarded visitation rights if the parent who is the child of the grandparent is deceased, incarcerated or has been "interdicted," meaning declared legally incompetent. In addition, in the case of death or incarceration, grandparents may petition for visitation if the parents of the child lived "in concubinage"—that is, are unmarried. Visitation may also be possible if the parents of the child are legally separated or living apart for a period of six months. As always, the court "in its discretion" must consider the best interest of the child. See LSA R.S. 9:344.

Article 136 of the Civil Code gives visitation rights, under extraordinary circumstances, to relatives by blood or affinity, including grandparents. Where this article conflicts with the first statute, the provisions of R.S. 9:344 supersede Article 136. Before granting visitation under Article 136, the court must consider the longevity and quality of the relationship; the relative's ability to provide needed guidance; the preference of the child, if the child is able to express a preference; the relative's willingness to promote the child's relationship with the parent; and the mental and physical health of both the child and the relative.

The final statute which is applicable is Article 1264 of the Children's Code, which decrees that grandparents lose visitation rights in the case of adoption unless the grandparents are the parents of a deceased parent or a parent who has forfeited his or her right to object to adoption.

Maine

Maine laws governing grandparent visitation are quite narrow and detailed. Visitation rights are based on one of the child's parents being deceased. The grandparent must prove a "sufficient existing relationship" or a sufficient effort to establish such a relationship. It is stipulated that grandparent visitation cannot interfere with the parent's relationship with the child or impair the parent's "rightful authority."

In awarding visitation, the court must consider a number of factors, including the following:

The age of the child

The grandparent-child relationship

The preference of the child, if old enough to express a preference

The child's current living arrangements and the desirability of maintaining continuity

The stability of any proposed living arrangements for the child

The motivation of the parties involved and their capacities to give the child love, affection and guidance

The child's adjustment to the existing situation

The capacity of the parent and grandparent to cooperate in child care

The willingness of both parties to resolve disputes

Any other factor impacting the physical and psychological well-being of the child.

The court is also instructed to consider a grandparent's conviction for a sex offense, though such a conviction does not automatically disqualify the grandparent from visitation.

Maine statutes provide for the appointment of a guardian ad litem for the child if deemed necessary. The court may also refer the parties to mediation. Adoption cuts off all visitation rights of grandparents.

Maryland

Maryland statutes address the subject of grandparent visitation in a single sentence, which simply states that a court may grant "reasonable visitation" to a grandparent if it is in the best interests of the child. The statute does not provide any means of determining the best interests of the child. Those criteria have been set forth in case law.

One of the important cases in Maryland is Koshko v. Haining. In this case, the Maryland statute was challenged by the parents as unconstitutional under Troxel v. Granville, which states that there is a presumption that fit parents make decisions that are in the best interests of their children. The Maryland Court of Appeals found that this presumption is "implicit" in the Maryland statute. The court further stated that in order for this presumption to be negated, there must be a finding of parental unfitness or "exceptional circumstances." The exceptional circumstances require a finding that a lack of grandparent visitation would have a detrimental effect upon the child. See Maryland statute. Look for Section 9.102. See also Koshko v. Haining.

Grandparents may receive visitation rights if the child's parents have divorced or separated, if a parent is deceased, or if the child was born out of wedlock but paternity has been established. Establishment of paternity is not required by visitation by the maternal grandparents. The best interests of the child must be considered, but no factors are given by statute for determining best interest. Several cases have addressed the issue, notably Blixt v. Blixt, Guardianship of Norman, and Sher v. Desmond. Adoption ends grandparents rights unless the adopting party is a stepparent. See Massachusetts statute.

Michigan

Following the U.S. Supreme Court finding in Troxel v. Granville, the Michigan Supreme Court in the 2003 case of Derose v. Derose declared its grandparent visitation law unconstitutional. New laws were passed in 2005. These laws are lengthy and detailed.

According to the new statutes, courts may award visitation—called "grandparenting time"—to grandparents if the parents of the grandchild are divorced, separated or have had their marriage annulled, or if such an action is pending. In addition, grandparents may receive visitation if a parent is deceased, if the child's parents are unmarried but paternity has been established or if custody of the child has been given to a third party. In the case of unmarried parents, paternal grandparents may request visitation only if the father has provided "substantial and regular support or care." In addition, if "two fit parents" file an affidavit opposing grandparenting time, the court may not award visitation. This provision does not apply if one of the parents is a stepparent who has adopted the child, and the grandparent is the natural or adoptive parent of a deceased parent or a parent whose parental rights have been terminated.

Michigan law also provides criteria for determining the best interest of the child, including the emotional ties between grandparent and grandchild, the prior relationship, the grandparent's "moral fitness," the grandparent's physical and mental health, any history of abuse of any child by the grandparent and any other factors affecting the child's well-being. In addition, the court must consider the effect on the child of any hostility existing between grandparent and parent and the willingness of the grandparent to support the parent-child relationship. Adoption terminates visitation rights unless the adopting party is a stepparent.

Minnesota

Visitation rights may be petitioned for in Minnesota during or after proceedings dealing with divorce, separation, custody, annulment and paternity. The courts are instructed to consider the prior relationship between the grandparent and grandchild and the impact of visitation on the parent-child relationship. In the case of a child with a deceased parent, the parents and grandparents of the deceased parent can request visitation, with the same two factors to be considered. In addition, a petition for visitation rights can be filed independently of one of the preceding actions if the grandchild has lived with the grandparent for at least a year and was removed from the grandparent's home by the parent. Great-grandparents are expressly mentioned in two sections of the statutes, the ones dealing with a child with a deceased parent and the one dealing with children who have lived with a grandparent for a year or more.

In the state of Minnesota, adoption cuts off visitation rights unless the adopting party is a stepparent.

See Minnesota statutes 518.1752 and 257C.08

Mississippi

The state of Mississippi allows grandparents to petition for visitation if they are the parents of a non-custodial parent, a parent whose parental rights have been terminated or a deceased parent. A grandparent may petition for visitation outside of the above circumstances only if there is a "viable" grandparent-grandchild relationship and if the grandparent has been "unreasonably" denied visitation. The statutes provide two tests for proving a viable relationship. The first is providing part or all of a child's financial support for at least six months. The second is having frequent visits with the child, including occasional overnight visits, for a period of at least one year.

In Mississippi, as in all of the 50 states, the courts must consider the best interest of the child. Mississippi statutes do not enumerate any factors to be considered in determining best interest, but in the case of Martin v. Koop, the Mississippi Supreme Court listed ten factors. These include:

Any disruption caused by visitation
The suitability of the grandparent's home
The age of the child

The age and both the physical and mental health of the grandparents

Any emotional ties between grandparent and grandchild

The grandparent's moral fitness

The physical distance between the child's home and the grandparent's

Any undermining of the parent's discipline by the grandparent

Any responsibilities associated with the employment of the grandparent

The grandparent's willingness to accept the parent's child-rearing decisions.

Grandparents may not file for visitation with a child who has been adopted unless one of the adoptive parents is a natural parent or unless one of the adoptive parents was related to the child by blood or marriage prior to the adoption.

Missouri

Grandparents in the state of Missouri may intervene in a divorce suit to request visitation. Outside of a divorce suit, the grandparents must have been denied visitation. Grandparents who have been denied visitation can file a petition in the following cases:

The parents are divorced

One parent is deceased and the other denied visitation

The grandparent has been "unreasonably" denied visitation for 90 days or more.

However, if the natural parents are legally married to each other and are living together with the child, a grandparent may not file for visitation under this provision.

Missouri law favors what are sometimes called intact families by stating that if the child's natural parents are legally married and living with the child, they know what is in the best interest of the child. This provision is what as known as a "rebuttable presumption," meaning that in the instance of denied visitation, grandparents will have the burden of proving that it is not true. As in all states, courts are instructed to consider the child's best interest. Missouri statutes allow the court to appoint a guardian ad litem, order a home study or consult with the child in order to determine the child's best interest.

Adoption puts an end to grandparents rights unless the adopting party is a stepparent, a grandparent or a blood relative.

Montana

Grandparents in the state of Montana may petition for "reasonable rights to contact" with a grandchild regardless of the status of the child's parents. If a parent whose parental rights have not been terminated objects to such contact, the grandparent's task becomes more difficult.

One way to win visitation over the wishes of a parent is to present "clear and convincing evidence" of the parent's unfitness. In order to prove unfitness, a grandparent must prove one of the conditions enumerated in a separate statute, 42-2-608. These include:

A parent has lost custody due to abuse or neglect

The parent has abandoned the child

The parent, although able, has not contributed to the child's support for a year

The parent is in violation of an order to support the child or another child of the same birth mother

The parent has been found guilty of a crime against a child, including aggravated assault, sexual assault, sexual intercourse without consent, incest, homicide, sexual abuse or ritual abuse.

The child has been maintained by a public or private agency for one year without the parent contributing to the child's support, if able

The parent has been convicted of a crime or of violating a protective order, indicating that the parent is unfit.

Even if a parent is proven unfit, the grandparents must still present evidence that contact is in the best interests of the child. If a parent is considered fit, a grandparent may win the right to contact with the grandchild over parental objections if "clear and convincing evidence" is presented that the contact with the grandparent would be in the best interest of the child and that the presumption in favor of the parent's wishes has been rebutted.

Petitions for grandparent-grandchild contact cannot be presented more often than once every two years unless something about the grandchild's situation has changed. The court may appoint an attorney to represent the interests of the child if it deems necessary. Adoption terminates the rights of the grandparents unless the adopting party is a stepparent or grandparent.

Nebraska

Grandparents in Nebraska may petition for visitation if at least one of the child's parents is deceased, if the marriage of the parents has been dissolved or a petition for dissolution is pending, or if the child's parents have never been married but paternity has been legally established. The grandparent must file an affidavit offering evidence that a "significant beneficial relationship exists, or has existed in the past." As in all of the United States, the court must find that the grandparent-grandchild relationship is in the best interest of the child. In addition, the court must find that that visitation will not "adversely interfere" with the relationship between parent and child. The court may modify a visitation order if there is a "material change" in the child's circumstances.

Nebraska law does not cite factors to be considered in determining the best interest of the child, but an annotation to the statute mentions several relevant court cases. In one of these cases, Raney v. Blecha, the finding was that adoption does not automatically end grandparent visitation rights.

Nevada

Grandparents who are the parents of a non-custodial parent or of a deceased parent may seek visitation with a grandchild in the state of Nevada. The child's parents need not have been married if they cohabitated. Grandparents may also seek visitation if the parent's rights have been terminated or relinquished. In all of these situations, however, the custodial or surviving parent must have denied or "unreasonably restricted" visitation.

The decision of the parent to restrict visitation is presumed to be in the best interests of the child, but this is a rebuttable presumption. The State of Nevada sets out special criteria for determining the best interest of the child. These include:

Emotional ties existing between the grandparent and grandchild

The grandparent's ability to provide love and guidance and serve as a role model

The grandparent's willingness to supply material needs during visitation

The grandparent's ability to provide the child with health care

The prior relationship between the two, including such factors as whether the grandchild resided with the grandparent and whether the child was present at holidays and family gatherings

The grandparent's moral fitness

the grandparent's mental and physical health

The preference of the child, if applicable

The willingness of the grandparent to facilitate and encourage the child-parent relationship

The medical needs of the child

Any financial or other support provided by the grandparent

Any other pertinent facts

The same criteria outlined for grandparents also applies to great-grandparents, siblings and any person with whom the child has resided and has established a meaningful relationship.

Adoption does not always end visitation rights. The request for visitation rights must have been filed before the parental rights were relinquished, and the court must, of course, determine that visitation is in the best interests of the child.

New Hampshire

In New Hampshire, both adoptive and natural grandparents may petition the court for "reasonable" visitation with a grandchild, provided that access to the child has not been restricted for any reason. In considering whether visitation would be in the best interest of the child, the court will also consider the following:

Whether visitation would interfere with the parent-child relationship or with parental authority

The nature of the grandparent-grandchild relationship, including the frequency of contact, any time of residence with the grandparent and the length of time of any such residence

Whether the child's physical and emotional health would be endangered by such visitation or lack of it

The relationship between the grandparent and the parent of the child, including friction between the grandparent and the parent, and the effect on the child of such friction

The circumstances which resulted in the "absence of a nuclear family," including divorce, death, termination or relinquishment of parental rights, or other circumstances

The guardian ad litem's recommendation, if one was appointed

The child's wishes

Any other factors which the court deems relevant.

If the grandchild's parents are not married, legitimacy or paternity must be attached to the petition seeking visitation. Adoption terminates the rights of the grandparents to visitation in New Hampshire.

New Jersey

A grandparent requesting visitation in the state of New Jersey bears the burden of proving "by a preponderance of the evidence" that visitation is in the best interests of the child. In determining the best interests, the court considers the following:

The relationship between the child and the grandparent

The relationship between the grandparent and each of the child's parents or the person with whom the child is residing

The time elapsed since the last contact with the grandparent

How visitation will affect the relationship between the child and the child's parents or the person with whom the child is residing

Any time-sharing arrangement which exists between divorced or separated parents with regard to the child

The grandparent's "good faith" in filing the application

Any history of abuse or neglect by the grandparent

Any other relevant factor.

If the grandparent has been a full-time caretaker for the grandchild in the past, that is *prima facie* evidence that visitation would be in the child's best interest. *Prima facie* evidence appears to be sufficient to prove an allegation; however, it can be rebutted. Adoption terminates the right to visitation unless the adopting party is a stepparent.

New Mexico

In New Mexico, grandparents may be awarded visitation during or following a court proceeding pertaining to paternity, legal separation, or dissolution of a marriage. Grandparent visitation must not conflict with the child's education, prior established visitation or time-sharing privileges. If either or both parents are deceased, any grandparent of the child may petition for visitation privileges. In addition, grandparents may petition for visitation with a grandchild who once resided with the grandparent for a prescribed length of time. For children who were less than six years old at the beginning of the residence, a period of three months or more is required. For children who were more than six years old at the beginning of the residence, a period of six months or more is required.

New Mexico statutes list items to be considered in a petition for grandparent visitation. These include the following:

Fact ors relevant to the best interests of the child

Prior grandparent-child interaction

Prior interaction between the grandparent and each parent of the child

The present relationship between the grandparent and each parent of the child

Any time-sharing or visitation arrangements already in place

The effect the visitation will have on the child

If the grandparent has any prior convictions for physical, emotional or sexual abuse or neglect

If the grandparent has been the child's full-time caretaker for a significant period.

The court may order mediation or evaluation if it is deemed advisable. If the court decides against visitation, it may order other grandparent-grandchild contact, including regular communication by phone, mail or "other reasonable means."

Adoption does not always terminate visitation rights in New Mexico. Biological grandparents may petition for visitation if the adopting party is a stepparent, a relative, a person designated in a deceased parent's will or a person sponsoring the child in baptism or confirmation ceremonies.

New York

The New York provisions regarding grandparent visitation are among the briefest in the 50 states, yet they are not easy to understand. For one thing, visitation and custody are treated in the same statute. For another, the language is more legalistic than that of some states.

Basically New York law provides for grandparent visitation if at least one parent is deceased. The only other condition mentioned in the statute is "where circumstances show that conditions exist which equity would see fit to intervene." As in all of the 50 states, visitation must be in the best interest of the child. Those wanting more insight into the workings of the law in New York should read Five Critical Issues in New York's Grandparent Visitation Law After Troxel v. Granville by Stephen A. Newman, which references the most important examples of case law.

North Carolina

Grandparents in North Carolina may be granted visitation in any order pertaining to custody of a child. See North Carolina General Statutes, Section 50-13.2.

Visitation can be granted after adoption if the adopting party is a stepparent or relative and if a "substantial relationship" exists between grandparent and grandchild.

North Dakota

Grandparents, including great-grandparents, in North Dakota may be granted "reasonable visitation rights" if the court finds that visitation would be in the best interests of the child and would not interfere with the parent-child relationship. The court is directed to consider the amount of personal contact that has occurred between the grandparents or great-grandparents and the child and the child's parents.

Ohio

In Ohio, grandparents may be granted visitation as part of a divorce, dissolution of marriage, legal separation, annulment, or child support proceeding. The court may grant "reasonable companionship or visitation rights" to any grandparent with an interest in the child's welfare, as determined by the court, if such visitation is in the best interest of the child. Such visitation rights are not limited to grandparents but may be sought by "any person related to the child by consanguinity or affinity," with the same conditions applying.

The court should consider factors including but not limited to the following:

The geographical location of the grandparent's residence and the distance from the child's residence

The child's and parents' available time, including schedules for employment, school, holidays and vacations

The child's age

The child's adjustment at home and school and in the community

Any wishes of the child, as expressed in chambers
The child's health and safety
The availability of time for the child to be with his or her siblings
The mental and physical health of all parties
The willingness of the grandparent to reschedule missed visitation
Any conviction of the grandparent or guilty plea by the grandparent involving a crime of child abuse or child neglect
The wishes and concerns of the parents as expressed to the court
Any other factor in the best interest of the child.

A grandparent who is the parent of a deceased parent may seek visitation with a grandchild who is the child of the deceased. In the case of unmarried parents, grandparents may seek visitation, although paternity must be acknowledged and legalized before paternal grandparents may seek visitation. In cases involving deceased parents or unmarried parents, the court is instructed to consider the same factors listed above. Visitation rights may survive after adoption if the adopting party is a stepparent.

Oklahoma

Oklahoma law governing grandparent visitation is extremely long and detailed, though relatively clear and easy to understand. In Oklahoma, grandparents may be granted visitation if the court deems it in the best interest of the child, provided that the grandparent can show either parental unfitness, or that the child would suffer harm in the absence of visitation. Visitation will not be awarded under any circumstances if the nuclear family is intact and both parents object to visitation. Family situations in which visitation can be sought include death, divorce, separation, annulment, unmarried parents, incarceration and desertion. In most of these situations, a preexisting relationship between the grandparent and the grandchild is necessary for visitation. Some of the subsections call for a "strong, continuous grandparental relationship."

Oklahoma law provides factors for consideration in deciding the best interests of the child. These include the following:

The importance to the child of continuing a preexisting relationship with the grandparent

The age and reasonable preference of the child

the willingness of the grandparent to encourage a close parent-child relationship

the length, quality and intimacy of the preexisting grandparental relationship

The emotional ties between the parent and child

The motivation and efforts of the grandparent to continue the grandparental relationship

The parental motivation for denying visitation

The mental and physical health of the grandparent

The mental and physical health of the child

The mental and physical health of the parent

The permanence and stability of the family unit and environment

The moral fitness of the parties

The character and behavior of any other person who resides in or frequents the homes of the parties

the quantity of visitation time requested and any adverse impact it would have on the child's customary activities

If both parents are dead, the benefit in maintaining the preexisting relationship.

Oklahoma also provides guidelines for proving parental unfitness in a suit for grandparent visitation; however, such a finding cannot be used to terminate parental rights. These factors include the following:

Chemical or alcohol dependency, untreated or unsuccessfully treated

A history of violent behavior or domestic abuse

An emotional or mental illness that impairs judgment or impairs the capacity to recognize reality or to control behavior

A failure to provide the child with proper care, guidance and support

Any other condition making the parent unable or unwilling to give a child reasonable parental care.

Adoption does not automatically terminate grandparents rights in Oklahoma as it does in some states. The law states that visitation may be sought if a grandchild is not living with the parents or if legal custody has been given to another party, except in some cases of legal adoption. Grandparents of a legally adopted child cannot request visitation after the adoption or in a case in which a child was adopted before the age of six months. Visitation rights that were awarded before the adoption may not be terminated without an action of the court. Great-grandparents have the same right to visitation as grandparents.

Oregon

The statutes of Oregon providing for visitation rights are not limited to grandparents but include any person who has emotional ties with a child that have created a child-parent relationship or an "ongoing personal relationship." The statute defines a child-parent relationship as existing in whole or in part within the six months preceding the filing of a request for visitation. In this relationship, the person should have had physical custody, resided in the same house, or otherwise provided for the child's daily needs, meeting "the child's psychological need for a parent as well as the child's physical needs." The statute defines an "ongoing personal relationship" as one with "substantial continuity for at least one year," featuring "interaction, companionship, interplay and mutuality." As is usual, the parents are presumed to have acted in the best interest of the child in refusing visitation, and the person seeking visitation must rebut that presumption. In deciding whether to award visitation or contact rights over the objection of the legal parent, the court may consider factors including the following:

The grandparent is or recently has been the child's primary caretaker.

Denying the request for visitation would be detrimental to the child.

The relationship between the grandparent and the child has been encouraged or consented to by the parent.

Visitation would not interfere with the custodial relationship.

The legal parent has unreasonably denied or limited visitation.

In deciding whether deciding whether the presumption of parents acting in the child's best interest has been rebutted, the court may consider the same factors, considering as well whether the legal parent is unwilling or unable to care for the child. Adoption terminates visitation rights.

Pennsylvania

Grandparents in Pennsylvania may seek visitation or "reasonable partial custody" if a parent of the child has died or if the parents are divorced or have been separated for six months or more. The court is instructed to consider the amount of personal contact that took place before the application. In addition, if the child resided with the grandparent for twelve months or more and was removed from the grandparent's home by parents, the court may rule in favor of visitation. As in all of the United States, the court must consider whether visitation is in the child's best interest. In addition, in Pennsylvania, the court must consider whether visitation would interfere with the parent-child relationship. Great-grandparents have the same rights as parents. Adoption terminates visitation rights unless the adopting party is a stepparent or grandparent.

Rhode Island

Before Rhode Island grandparents can be awarded visitation rights, the courts must find such visitation is in the best interest of the grandchild. That is standard in all 50 states. In addition, in Rhode Island the court must find that the grandparent is a "fit and proper person" to have contact with the child, that the grandparent has repeatedly attempted visitation during the 90 days preceding the filing of the petition, that visitation was not allowed as a result of parental action and that the grandparent cannot visit the grandchild without court intervention. Moreover, to bring the state into compliance with the U.S. Supreme Court case of Troxel v. Granville, the grandparent must offer "clear and convincing evidence" to rebut the presumption that the parent's decision to refuse the grandparent visitation was reasonable. Adoption cuts off visitation rights in Rhode Island.

South Carolina

In the state of South Carolina, the courts have the power to order grandparent visitation if a parent is deceased or if parents are divorced or living separately. As in all of the 50 states, the court must find that visitation would be in the best interests of the child. In addition, the court must find that visitation would not interfere with the parent-child relationship. The court is also directed to consider the nature of the relationship between the child and the grandparents prior to the filing of the request for visitation. Visitation rights are terminated upon adoption.

South Dakota

In South Dakota, the circuit court may grant grandparents reasonable rights of visitation with their grandchild, with or without petition by the grandparents. As in all of the 50 states, the court must find visitation to be in the best interests of the grandchild. In addition, in South Dakota, the court must make one of the two following findings:

That the child's parent or guardian has denied visitation or has prevented the grandparent from having a "reasonable opportunity" for visitation

That the visitation will not "significantly interfere" with the parent-child relationship.

The term grandparents includes great-grandparents. Grandparents rights of visitation terminate upon the adoption of a grandchild, unless the adopting party is a stepparent or grandparent.

Tennessee

Tennessee's statutes regarding grandparent visitation are lengthy and complex. In Tennessee, any of the following circumstances necessitates a hearing if visitation is requested by a grandparent and opposed by the custodial parent:

The father or mother is deceased

The child's father or mother are divorced, legally separated, or were never married to each other

A parent of the child has been missing for at least six months

The child resided in the home of the grandparent for twelve months or more and was subsequently removed from the home by the parent, establishing a rebuttable presumption that denial of visitation may result in irreparable harm to the child

There has been a "significant existing relationship" for at least twelve months between the grandparent and grandchild. This relationship was terminated by the parent, not for reason of abuse or endangerment, with this severance being likely to cause "substantial emotional harm" to the child.

In considering a petition for grandparent visitation, the court shall first determine whether cessation of the grandparent-grandchild relationship might cause substantial harm to the child. The court will consider whether the grandparent functioned as a primary caregiver, so that interruption of the relationship could cause interruption of provisions for the child's daily needs. In addition, the court shall consider whether the "significant existing relationship" with the grandparent was such that cessation would cause "severe emotional harm" to the child or other "direct and substantial harm." The court must find that a "significant existing relationship" exists if the child resided with the grandparent for at least six months, if the grandparent was a full-time caretaker for at least six months or if the grandparent had frequent visitation with the child for at least one year. The grandparents are not expected to present expert witnesses. Instead, the court shall consider whether the facts of the particular case would lead a reasonable person to believe that there is a significant existing relationship between the grandparent and grandchild or that the loss of the relationship is likely to occasion severe emotional harm to the child. If after hearing the evidence, the court decides that visitation would be in the best interests of the child, the court shall order reasonable visitation. The term grandparent includes biological grandparents and their spouses and the parents of adoptive parents. If a person other than a relative or a stepparent adopts a child, any visitation rights granted will automatically end.

Texas

In Texas a court may award a grandparent "reasonable possession of or access to" a grandchild as long as least one biological or adoptive parent still has parental rights. The grandparent must "overcome the presumption" that a parent barring access is acting in the best interest of the child. In order to overcome this presumption, the grandparent must prove that denial would "significantly impair the child's physical health or emotional well-being."

In Texas the grandparent requesting access to a grandchild must be the parent of a parent who is dead, incarcerated, has been found by a court to be incompetent or for other reason does not have "actual or court-ordered possession of or access to the child."

A grandparent may not request access to a grandchild if both biological parents are dead or have had parental rights terminated. In addition, grandparents may not gain access if the grandchild has been adopted by other than a stepparent, or if both parents have executed affidavits designating another person or an agency as "managing conservator" of the child.

Utah

Utah law refers to the "rebuttable presumption" that a parent's decision about grandparent visitation is in the best interest of the child. The Utah Code lists several factors relevant to rebutting the presumption. These include the following:

Whether the grandparent is a fit and proper person to have visitation rights

Whether visitation with the grandchild has been denied or "unreasonably limited"

Whether the parent is unfit or incompetent

Whether the grandparent has served as custodian or caregiver to the grandchild, or otherwise has had such a substantial relationship with the child that cessation of the relationship would harm the grandchild.

Whether the grandparent's child has died or become a noncustodial parent through divorce or legal separation

Whether the parent who is the child of the grandparent has been missing for an extended period of time.

As in all of the fifty states, the courts must consider whether visitation is in the best interest of the child. The court may interview the child and take into account his or her wishes. Adoption terminates visitation rights unless the adopting party is a stepparent.

Vermont

Grandparents in Vermont may request visitation with a grandchild if a parent is deceased, physically or mentally incapable of making a decision or has abandoned the child. As in all fifty states, the court must find that visitation would be in the best interests of the child. Factors to be considered when determining best interests include the following:

The emotional ties between grandparent and grandchild

The ability of the grandparent to provide love, affection and guidance

The nature of the grandparent-grandchild relationship and the desirability of maintaining it

The moral fitness of the parties

The mental and physical health of the parties

The "reasonable preference" of the child, when the child is old enough to express a preference

The willingness of the grandparent to encourage and facilitate a close relationship between the child and the other parties

Any other factor considered by the court to be relevant to a "just determination" regarding visitation.

Visitation rights expire upon the adoption of the grandchild, unless the adopting party is a stepparent, grandparent or other relative.

Virginia

In the state of Virginia, determining grandparents visitation rights is complicated by the fact that there is no statute dedicated to those rights. Instead Virginia addresses custody and visitation in the same set of statutes. The statutes refer to parents and to "persons of legitimate interest," including but not limited to grandparents, stepparents, former stepparents, blood relatives and family members. A grandparent who is the parent of a parent whose parental rights have been terminated is not considered a person of legitimate interest. Adoption terminates grandparents rights unless the adopting party is a stepparent. Tools available to the court include mediation, independent mental health or psychological evaluation and on-camera interviews with the child, although such tools are probably more likely to be used in cases involving parental custody and visitation than they are in cases involving grandparents.

The court is also instructed to "give due regard to the primacy of the parent-child relationship."

"Clear and convincing evidence that the best interest of the child would be served" is required for custody or visitation to be awarded to "any other person with a legitimate interest." The factors to be considered in determining best interest are listed in the statutes, but some do not apply to grandparent visitation. The full list is as follows:

The age and physical and mental condition of the child, with consideration given to developmental needs

The age and physical and mental condition of each parent

The relationship between each parent and each child, with consideration given to parental involvement and capability of meeting the emotional, intellectual and physical needs of the child

The needs of the child, giving due consideration to other important relationships of the child, including but not limited to siblings, peers and extended family members

The role that each parent has played and will play in the future, in the upbringing and care of the child

The propensity of each parent to actively support the child's contact and relationship with the other parent, including any unreasonable denial of access to the child

The willingness and demonstrated ability of each parent to maintain a close and continuing relationship with the child, and to cooperate in and resolve disputes about the child

The reasonable preference of the child, if the court deems the child able to express such a preference

Any history of family abuse

Any other factors deemed necessary and proper by the court.

Washington

Washington State is currently the only state without an operational statute for grandparent visitation. The Washington statute is still on the books, but it was found unconstitutional by the Washington Supreme Court in 2005. Efforts to pass statutes governing grandparent visitation failed in 2006.

It was the Washington State's visitation law that the U.S. Supreme Court struck down as "breathtakingly broad" in the 2000 landmark case of Troxel v. Granville, casting doubt on the visitation laws of almost every state. In Washington State, the law was amended, but found unconstitutional by the Washington Supreme Court in 2005 in the case "In re Parentage of C.A.M.A."

The court stated that the statute "unconstitutionally infringes on a fit parent's right to control visitation." The Washington Supreme Court did, however, acknowledge the custody and visitation rights of "de facto" parents, which can be applicable to some grandparents. To show that one is a de facto parent requires the following:

The natural or legal parent consented to and fostered the parent-like relationship

The petitioner and the child lived together in the same household

The petitioner assumed obligations of parenthood without expectation of financial compensation

The petitioner has been in a parental role for a length of time sufficient to have established with the child a bonded, dependent relationship, parental in nature.

In the case of "In re Parentage of L.B." Washington court stated that a de facto parent is not entitled to parental privileges as a matter of right but only when the granting of such privileges is determined to be in the best interests of the child.

West Virginia

The West Virginia Code is quite lengthy and complex, spelling out factors for determining the best interest of the child as well as the differing standards required for grandparent visitation in different situations.

In West Virginia, the courts must find not only that visitation by a grandparent would be in the best interests of the child, as in all 50 states, but also that such visitation would not "substantially interfere with the parent-child relationship." The following factors are to be considered in awarding grandparent visitation:

The child's age

The grandchild-grandparent relationship

The relationship between each of the child's parents or the person with whom the child is residing and the grandparent

The time which has elapsed since the child last had contact with the grandparent

The possible effect of visitation on the relationship between the child and the child's parents or the person with whom the child is residing

In the case of parents who are divorced or separated, the custody and visitation arrangement which exists between the parents

The time available to the child and his or her parents, considering each parent's employment schedule, the child's schedule for home, school and community activities, and the child's and parents' holiday and vacation schedule

The good faith of the grandparent in filing the motion or petition

Any history of physical, emotional or sexual abuse or neglect being performed, procured, assisted or condoned by the grandparent

Whether the child has resided with the grandparent for a significant period of time, with or without the child's parent or parents

Whether the grandparent has, in the past, been a significant caretaker for the child

The preference of the parents

Any other factor relevant to the best interests of the child.

The child may be interviewed in chambers about his or her preference about grandparent visitation. The child is not to be called as a witness or asked to give a written or recorded statement about his or her preference about grandparent visitation.

As in all 50 states, visitation must be shown to be in the best interest of the child. The standard of proof required to prove best interest depends upon the family situation of the child. If the parent through whom the grandparent is related to the child does not have custody or visitation rights or is absent, all that is required for grandparent visitation to be awarded is "a preponderance of evidence" that visitation is in the child's best interest. If the parent through whom the grandparent is related to the grandchild has custody or shares custody or has visitation rights, the assumption is that the parent could provide time for the grandparent to be with the child. If the parent chooses not to provide that time, the presumption is that the parent believes that contact with the grandparent is not in the best interest of the child. This presumption must be rebutted with "clear and convincing evidence" that visitation is in the child's best interest. At the court's discretion, grandparent visitation can be required to be supervised. Other conditions can be placed on visitation, such as the grandparent being required not to influence the grandchild's religious beliefs, encourage any activities contrary to the parents' preferences or act contrary to any child-rearing decisions made by the parents. A grandparent can be found guilty of a misdemeanor if he or she allows contact between the grandchild and any person who has been denied visitation. Adoption terminates grandparent visitation rights unless the adopting party is a stepparent, grandparent or other relative.

Wisconsin

Wisconsin law addresses grandparent visitation rights in several different areas of the law. It specifically addresses visitation by a person who has maintained a relationship similar to a parent-child relationship, visitation by a grandparent who is the parent of a deceased parent and visitation in the case of stepparent adoption. The Wisconsin statutes were amended in 2005, and grandparents need to be sure that they are consulting the updated versions of the law. In addition to the statutes addressing these situations, several court cases have had an impact on grandparent visitation in the state of Wisconsin. An unusual provision of the Wisconsin statutes is that they specify that visitation cannot be granted to a person who has been convicted of homicide; although it is also provided that such a conviction can be ignored in the face of "clear and convincing evidence" that visitation is in the best interest of the child. In summary, grandparents wishing to file for visitation in the state of Wisconsin will almost certainly need comprehensive legal advice. The information here can provide only a broad outline of Wisconsin law.

Wisconsin Statute 767.43, formerly 767.245, provides for "reasonable visitation rights" for grandparents, great-grandparents or other persons who have maintained a relationship with a child that is similar to a parent-child relationship. The court is directed to act in the best interest of the child and to consider the wishes of the child whenever possible. A special grandparent visitation provision pertains to "non-marital" children. This special provision does not require the presence of a parent-child relationship for a grandparent to win visitation. Instead, the grandparent must have maintained a relationship with the child or must have attempted a relationship with the child but been prevented from doing so by the child's custodial parent. In addition to considering the best interest of the child, the court must also be satisfied as to the paternity of the child and must also find that the grandparent will abide by decisions made by the child's parents concerning the child's "physical, emotional, educational or spiritual welfare." See full text of 767.43.

Wisconsin Statute 54.56, formerly 880.155, provides for grandparent visitation when one or both of the child's parents are deceased. Grandparents may petition for visitation even if the surviving parent or person with custody is married. The adoption of a child of a deceased parent does not terminate the grandparental visitation rights of the parents of the deceased. See full text of 54.56.

Wisconsin Statute 48.925 provides that in the case of the adoption of a child by a stepparent or other relative, "certain persons" have the right to request visitation. Those persons are relatives who have maintained a relationship similar to a parent-child relationship, a definition that includes some grandparents but excludes others. If a grandparent is included in this definition, the court must find that visitation is in the best interest of the child. In addition, the following findings must be made: that the petitioner will not undermine the relationship between the child and any parent or adoptive parent and that the grandparent will respect the decisions made by the child's parents concerning the child's "physical, emotional, educational or spiritual welfare."

Wyoming

In the state of Wyoming, one statute addresses grandparent visitation rights and another addresses caregiver visitation rights, which will pertain to some grandparents. In the first instance, a grandparent is allowed to bring an original suit against any person having custody of a grandchild. In the second instance, a caregiver may petition for visitation if he or she has been the child's primary caregiver for at least six months out of the preceding eighteen months. Both statutes require the court to find that visitation would be in the best interest of the child and would not substantially impair the rights of the parents. Both statutes provide that if a guardian ad litem is appointed, the petitioner is responsible for those fees and expenses. Neither grandparents nor caregivers can sue for visitation rights in the case of a child adopted by persons not related by blood to the child. Visitation rights may be amended or revoked if the custodial parent or guardian demonstrate

Custody

Under normal circumstances grandparents have no recognized right to seek custody of the child, due to a lack of standing. Without proper standing, granted by statute, the court will not hear a complaint from a grandparent seeking custody.

Emergency Custody

One area in which a grandparent has limited standing to seek custody is in emergency circumstances, such as the death of one parent, though other emergency circumstances could apply. While this is meant to be employed on a temporary basis and will be granted only because the other parent is immediately unavailable to take custody, the length of the temporary placement varies.

Guardians

Being the guardian of a grandchild does not necessarily grant a right to custody and while grandparents have no standing to seek custody of a grandchild, guardians do. For many grandparents this may require an intermediate step of being appointed guardian of a grandchild before petitioning for custody. To be appointed a guardian requires either a parent's right to the child being terminated, some emergency to justify temporary guardianship, or the child has been living with the grandparent and receives no aid from the parent. Once appointed guardian, a grandparent can seek custody.

Best Interests of the Child

Should a grandparent be able to assert standing under the law to bring a complaint for custody of the grandchild, the grandparent still needs to satisfy the statutory criteria that the placement of the child in the grandparent's custody is in the best interests of the child. Before bringing any action you would do well to familiarize yourself with just exactly what these criteria are.

http://definitions.uslegal.com/b/best-interest-of-the-child/

The best interest of the child is a standard used in family law to make decisions impacting a child in matters of adoption, child custody, guardianship, and visitation, among other issues. It is a subjective, discretionary test, in which all circumstances affecting the child are taken into account.

Grandparenting Time

While a grandparent has no generalized right to seek custody, under the law they do have the right to seek visitation, or grandparenting time, with a child. However, this right is limited. For the court to allow visitation, the grandparent must first demonstrate the child's parents are either separated or divorcing, or have already done so, or that the grandparent's child (mother or father of the grandchild) has died. Once one of these criteria is established the grandparent must then rebut the presumption that a fit parent's decision to deny grandparent visitation does not create a substantial risk of harm to the child. If those two things can be done, visitation will be granted.

Grandparents do have the right to go to the Probate and Family Court and file paper work to seek grandparent visitation on a minor child. In order to do this you will need to locate your local Probate and Family Court in the County where you live. If the minor child has Court orders on them from another Court you will need to go to the Court where any orders on the child exist to file your request for visits. Your son or daughter must have been declared the biological parent of the child you are requesting to visit. For example their name on the birth certificate or by Court order.

Go to Courthouse and complete the required forms. You will need to state and or prove why it is in the minor child's best interest to visit with you and why the child would be in harm or a disadvantage if the relationship did not continue. Once you complete the paperwork and make your statement why you should have visits you will need to serve both biological parents or the child's legal guardian with a copy of the forms you completed along with the Court date. Service of these forms needs to be done by a neutral party, constable or sheriff. Then you go to Court and present your case.

Grandparents do not need to be married to seek visitation.

By Linda T. French Attorney at Law

What can grandparents do to see their grandkids? Find out here from a family law attorney with more than 25 years of experience.

Before going to court, grandparents should make every effort to reach an agreement for visitation with the parents of the children. Only if you are unable to do so, should you apply for a court order.

Grandparents can join in an existing case between the parents, such as a divorce or legal separation or they can file an independent request with the court.

Grandparents cannot file a petition for visitation rights if the parents are married unless one of the following are true:
The parents are separated.
One parent has disappeared for over a month.
One parent joins in the petition for grandparent visitation.
The child does not live with either parent.
One parent has died and the other refuses to let the grandparent visit with the children.

Before the court will grant visitation, a judge must find that the grandparents and the grandchildren have a pre-existing relationship that has engendered a bond between them.

Getting the court to order grandparent visitation would be extremely difficult if the natural or adoptive parents agreed that the grandparent should not see the children or if one parent has sole legal and sole physical custody of the child and objects to the visitation.

http://www.aarp.org/family/grandparenting/articles/grandparent_visit_rights_update.html?CMP=KNC-360I-YAHOO-FAM&HBX_OU=51&HBX_PK=grandparent_visitation

In the seesaw battle to test grandparents' rights in child-visitation disputes, Hawaii's highest court in December reversed the momentum grandparents had recently regained. The ruling comes after decisions in 2006 in Pennsylvania, Colorado, and Utah, in which those states' supreme courts had sided with grandparents who were forced to sue for visits with their grandchildren.

In another twist before that, a U.S. Supreme Court ruling in a case from Washington State—decided in 2000—had sent grandparents' visitation rights reeling. Prior to the Washington case, grandparents across the country had a legal right to sue for visits with their grandchildren. But in 2000, the Supreme Court sharply curtailed those rights.

"Everything changed after that," said Barbara Jones, an attorney with the AARP Foundation litigation staff. In that case, the Supreme Court ruled that a broad visitation statute in Washington, which allowed even non-relatives legal standing, violated the constitutional rights of parents. In its ruling, the court beefed up parental rights. The high court ruled that laws that are narrowly written or construed to respect the best interest of the child might comport with the Constitution, Jones added.

Family law has been reverberating ever since. As of 2007, 23 state supreme courts have ruled on the constitutionality of their respective state's visitation statutes, according to Jeff Atkinson, adjunct professor of law at Chicago's DePaul University and author of the American Bar Association's "Guide to Marriage, Divorce & Families." Most courts have held that the laws are constitutional, at least when applied in certain circumstances. But, since 2000, top courts in Florida, Illinois, Iowa, Michigan, and Washington have held their respective state statutes unconstitutional.

Legislatures in some of those states and in many others reworked their visitation statutes "to give weight to the decisions the parents make," said Traci Truly, a Dallas family lawyer and author of "Grandparents' Rights." Many people gave up grandparents' rights for dead, truly noted, but "grandparent rights didn't die; it [visitation] survived."

Still, grandparents' legal standing is not as broad as it once was. "It is possible for grandparents to obtain visitation rights in certain circumstances," Atkinson said. Courts have recently sided with grandparents in cases involving the death or incarceration of a parent, for example, or with grandparents who have raised their grandchildren for a period of time only to be cut off suddenly from seeing their grandkids, or in other cases in which grandchildren would be harmed by not seeing their grandparents.

"AARP believes grandparents should have the right to petition the court" on matters of visitation, said Amy Goyer, national coordinator for the AARP Foundation's Grandparenting Program. She remarked, "It should be left up to the courts in terms of what is in the best interest of the child."

"The burden of proof is firmly on grandparents to show visitation is necessary," Atkinson added. In some states, the laws say the court should decide based on what is in the best interest of the child. In other states, grandparents have to prove that the grandchild would be harmed if prevented from seeing the grandparents. This latter standard, a tougher one for grandparents to meet, was the essence of the recent ruling in Hawaii.

That case involved the grandparents of a boy who lived with his mother, the couple's daughter, but not his father. After the grandson complained to his grandparents that his mother's boyfriend had beaten him, a police investigation found evidence of corporal punishment but concluded that legal intervention was unwarranted. The grandparents discussed the beatings with their daughter, who then terminated any visitation by them. The grandparents claim that in addition to their protection of their grandson and concern for his care, their visitation was supported by their grandson's father, who, though absent from the family, supported the boy financially.

AARP filed a friend-of-the-court, or amicus, brief in the case and emphasized studies showing the benefits of grandparents' involvement. Studies demonstrate that grandparents contribute significantly to the healthy development of their grandchildren. In cases where homes are broken by divorce, incarceration, mental and physical illness, AIDS, crime, or the death of one or both parents, Jones said, the presence of a constant and reliable family member, grandparent, or other relative, is particularly important to children.

AARP argued that the "best interest of the child" standard in the state's grandparents' visitation statute was the appropriate basis for which to award visitation, but the Hawaii Supreme Court ruled that the state's lower courts must adopt a test of whether upholding the parent's wishes could cause "harm" to the child.

Seeking a Better Alternative

The back-and-forth court rulings should give grandparents added incentive to try to work out issues or bad feelings with their grandchildren's parents, in order to see the grandkids.

"We urge people to resolve out of court," Jones said. Going to court should be a last-ditch option. "It's costly and takes years," she added, and can rip families further apart. If your attempts to resolve issues fail, consider using a trained mediator.

"We urge mediation first," Goyer said. A low-cost option, mediation helps people come to an agreement. Typically, each side gives a little, but each gains, too. To find a mediator in your area, check out the National Association for Community Mediation.

"We can help parents and grandparents work it out," said Mary Ellen Bowen, executive director of Mid-South Mediation Services in Hohenwald, Tenn.

If you have tried that avenue and find that going to court is the only option left, then contact a family lawyer to find out whether courts have upheld strong grandparents' visitation rights in the state where the child lives.

The words that resound throughout the law are a "fit parent". What is a fit parent? How is it determined that they are unfit? http://www.childwelfare.gov/systemwide/laws_policies/ statutes/best_interestall.pdf

The definition of an unfit parent is governed by state laws, which vary by state. A parent may be deemed unfit if they have been abusive, neglected, or failed to provide proper care for the child. A parent with a mental disturbance or addiction to drugs or alcohol may also be found to be an unfit parent. Failure to visit, provide support, or incarceration are other examples of grounds for being found unfit.

For example, one state declares the power of the juvenile court to terminate the rights of a natural parent (a) who was "unfit or incompetent by reason of conduct or condition seriously detrimental to the child," (b) who "abandoned the child," or (c) who "substantially and continuously or repeatedly refused or failed to give the child proper parental care and protection."

Some state laws provide for a fitness hearing to be held after an adjudication of neglect, dependency or abuse. In such cases, the law may specify a time period after such an adjudication in which the parent may make efforts to resolve the problem, such as seeking drug or alcohol treatment. A parent's failure to make reasonable efforts and progress within the specified time frame is a ground of unfitness. Local laws should be consulted for specific requirements in your area.

The court will often award sole custody to the other parent when one parent is deemed unfit, or if both parents are deemed unfit, the child may be placed in foster care. Evidence of parental unfitness toward one child may be grounds for terminating the parental rights to other children even though the parent never abused or neglected those children. The best interest of the child is the determining factor.

http://www.articlesbase.com/book-reviews-articles/

What is the definition of a "Fit" parent? No state law or court case has ever defined what a "Fit" parent is. Instead, courts attempt to define an "Unfit" parent.

Unfit parents come in different categories:

Parents who physically abuse their children by causing bodily harm are considered unfit.

Parents who cause mental or emotional harm to their children are also unfit.

Parents who actually cause or allow others to sexually abuse their children are unfit as well.

Failure to allow proper medical treatment whether because of religious or cultural beliefs have resulted in courts finding the parents to be unfit.

In determining the child's best interest, one court has stated that it shall consider, but is not limited to, the following circumstances:

(i) The willingness of the parent or parents to receive or care for the child; (ii) That the child has been removed from the custody of the parent by temporary order of the court for a period of six months and further finds that: (A) The conditions which led to the removal still exist; (B) There is little likelihood that those conditions will be remedied at an early date so that the child can be returned to the parent in the near future; and (C) The

continuation of the parent-child relationship greatly diminishes the child's prospects for early integration into a stable and permanent home...

Child Custody and custody battles can linger for a very long time until something is done through the court system. Grandparents and grandchildren are too often the victims of custody battles.

The "best interest of the child" is the legal test as set forth in PA Statutes Section 5301: "The General Assembly declares that it is the public policy of this Commonwealth, when in the best interest of the child, to assure a reasonable and continuing contact of the child with both parents after a separation or dissolution of the marriage and the sharing of the rights and responsibilities of child rearing by both parents andcontinuing contact of the child or children with grandparents when a parent is deceased, divorced or separated."

§ 5301. Declaration of policy.

http://www.uwex.edu/relationships/files/B3786-2.pdf

Bibliography:

kidshealth.org/teen/your_mind/emotions/stress.html
http://www.articlesbase.com/book-reviews-articles/
http://www.childwelfare.gov/systemwide/laws_policies/statutes/best_interestall.pdf
http://gerontologist.gerontologyjournals.org/cgi/content/abstract/45/2/262
http://www.wvu.edu/~exten/infores/pubs/fypubs/240.wlg.pdf)
http://www.vera.org/content/childhood-loss-and-behavioral-problems
http://www.ehow.com/about_5384528_custody-laws-grandparents.html
http://definitions.uslegal.com/b/best-interest-of-the-child/
http://www.aarp.org/family/grandparenting/articles/grandparent_visit_rights_update.html?CMP=KNC-360I-YAHOO-FAM&HBX_OU=51&HBX_PK=grandparent_visitation
http://www.childwelfare.gov/systemwide/laws_policies/statutes/best_interestall.pdf
Coping With Parental Loss Due to Termination of Parental Rights www.cwla.org
The Boy Who Was Raised As a Dog by Dr. Bruce Perry
http://www.ehow.com/how_5520659_obtain-grandparent-visitation-california.html